The Official Veganuary Cookbook

The Official Veganuary Cookbook

100 amazing vegan recipes for everyone!

Thorsons

CONTENTS

A LITTLE ABOUT US

Veganuary has been helping people all around the world try vegan – and stay vegan – through our month-long pledge since 2014. And while there are many good reasons to eat more plants, including for the animals, for our own health, and for that of the planet, few people would get past the first week if the food was not delicious.

And it is delicious. Or at least it can be. And easily! We truly believe that choosing vegan food is not about sacrifice. Quite the opposite; it's about abundance. It's about broadening our culinary horizons and discovering a world of beautiful ingredients and dishes that we may never have considered before. One of the most common comments we receive from Veganuary participants every year is: *I thought it would be restrictive, I thought I'd miss out, but I now eat a much wider range of foods than I ever have before.*

For many of us, it is too easy to fall into a food rut when life gets busy, and we get stuck cooking and eating the same seven dishes (or fewer) on repeat. With this book, we aim to help you clamber back out of that rut and discover a wealth of new meals that are simple but satisfying, often comforting, sometimes showstopping, and always delicious. So we have written a book that contains many timeless classics to prove you don't have to miss out on your old favourites when you eat vegan, alongside some new and innovative dishes to perk up your culinary life.

This book is not for vegans. At least, it's not intended *just* for vegans. It's for fledgling and wannabe vegans, flexitarians who want to eat more plants but need some inspiration, and for those who want to change their relationship with food or embark on a new journey of discovery without leaving home.

We don't expect you to have heard of every ingredient, although they are all easy to find, so we have created a reference section where you can see what everything is and where to get it later on in this chapter. And because we hate food waste, we have included ways to use up any perishable or unusual ingredients for you to refer back to whenever needed.

Many of our recipes are easily adaptable and we point out where you can switch out ingredients you don't have or don't like. It's no big deal.Change what you want. It's your meal, after all. So, flick through, dip in, and see what takes your fancy.

We hope you love trying these new dishes and putting more plants on your plate. For animals. For the planet. For you.

In kindness,

TEAM VEGANUARY

WHAT DO VEGANS EAT?

This is a question we get asked *a lot*. 'What do vegans eat for breakfast?' or 'What do vegans have for dinner?' But this is like asking, 'What do people eat?' It depends on many things, including our taste, preferences, culture, country, season, what we ate as children, whether we love to cook, what's available, what we fancy, how much time we have, who we are cooking for, and many other factors.

If we are honest, some days we eat half a pack of biscuits while our ready meal is spinning in the microwave; but other days you'll find us eating fresh and vibrant salads or covered in flour and whipping up a storm in the kitchen. In short, vegans are like everyone else, and mostly, we eat the same kinds of foods that non-vegans eat, just without the animal-based ingredients.

Breakfast could be toast and jam, porridge, or cereal and yoghurt, with some juice or a large mug of tea or coffee. Lunch may be soup or a wrap, sushi or sandwiches. And for dinner we may choose lasagne or sausage and mash, pizza or pasta. On a Friday night, we may pick up a takeaway or take the family out for a burger. See? We're entirely normal!

And vegans, like everyone else, have a life. We have to go to work, pick up the kids, walk the dogs and clean the bathroom. And somewhere within that, we need to get to the supermarket, shop, cook and feed ourselves. We know that life is busy and sometimes very challenging, so we want to reassure you that there is vegan food all around you and, even if you are not vegan, you are already eating it.

Take a look in your cupboards and refrigerator. You may see tinned tomatoes, chickpeas, baked beans, vegetable soup and coconut milk. There may be bread, crackers, peanut butter, jam, yeast extract, breakfast cereals, crumpets and porridge oats. You'll see pasta and rice, stock cubes and gravy granules, soy sauce, olive oil, mustard, ketchup, herbs and spices. And you'll find potatoes, salad vegetables, fruits and nuts, and there may be frozen oven chips and peas in the freezer too. So, when you add in a few vegan alternatives, such as plant milk, butter, yoghurt and cheese, and some veggie sausages, plant-based burgers and mince, it is easy to see that making your most-loved dishes is almost always possible as a vegan because those dishes already contain so many vegan ingredients.

This means that, at the supermarket, vegans are not restricted to the 'free from' section, although we certainly find some tasty items there. No, we roam all the aisles, and pick up the foods and ingredients that are vegan by default and sitting on the shelves for everyone to choose.

You may have noticed that many cuisines from around the world don't rely on meat, and where it is included, it is more of an optional extra. Your favourite curry – whether that's Indian or Thai – gets its rich flavours from the spices and other plant ingredients it is made with. And it's the same with many other cuisines, such as Lebanese, Italian, Mexican, Japanese and Chinese. So, when we become vegan, we can still enjoy all those flavours we have always loved and if we miss the meat, we can very easily add in vegan meat substitutes to those dishes.

So, what do vegans eat? Pretty much the same kinds of meals as everyone else.

WHY VEGAN?

While every vegan has their own motivations, three reasons for switching to a plant-based diet crop up over and over. For those of us who cannot bear the thought of factory farms and slaughterhouses, and how animals must suffer inside them, eating a diet free from meat, eggs and dairy is the way we withdraw our support from those industries. For those who care about the planet – its climate, wild places, wildlife, forests, oceans and rivers – being vegan is an immediate way to better protect and support our home, and the millions of other species that live in it. And for those who wish to reduce their own risk of chronic diseases,[1] while also tackling the twin public health threats of antibiotic resistance[2] and viral pandemics,[3] eating vegan is an obvious choice. But whatever reason motivates someone to *try* veganism in the first place often becomes just one of many reasons why they *stay* vegan.

For Animals

It is obvious that animals suffer and die for meat, but many people don't realise that cows that are kept for their milk and chickens that are reared for their eggs are also victims of the factory farm and slaughter industries. There is no happy retirement home for elderly cows and hens! When their bodies can no longer be monetised through milk or egg production, their lives are over.

Of the 70 billion animals reared and slaughtered every year, most are factory farmed. That means they are reared inside industrial facilities, fed artificial and processed foods, and have everything manipulated from their own bodies to the lighting to their fertility. Babies are taken from mothers; animals are locked inside crates and cages; legally sanctioned mutilations are commonplace; and animals are denied everything that could make their lives worth living. If they lived freely, they would roam and root in the earth, choose a mate, build a den or a nest, and rear their young. Birds would roost and fly; cows would roam and graze; pigs would dig up the earth looking for food; sheep would run nimbly across craggy landscapes, flocking together for protection and in friendship, safe from being rounded up for the slaughterers.

Polls show that most people believe themselves to be animal lovers and oppose factory farming. A large proportion also say that slaughterhouses should be banned. And yet we disconnect from it all when it comes to mealtimes. Often, all it takes is to see inside a farm, and to look into the eyes of an animal, even for a moment, even via an online video, and we instinctively know that what we see is not right. It is also not inevitable. Factory farms and slaughterhouses exist only because we fund them when we buy meat, milk and eggs. If we stop, they stop.

For the Planet

We have known for decades that the planet is heating up, and we have known for decades that the farming and consumption of meat, milk and eggs is helping to drive that change. The exact proportion of climate-altering gases released by animal agriculture is debated. The United Nations says it is around 14.5 per cent,[4] which is more than is pumped out by every car, bus, plane, train and ship on the planet. Others say the figure is much higher,[5] but what every credible institution agrees on – from Harvard and Oxford University to Chatham House and the United Nations[6] – is that to tackle climate breakdown, we need to eat plant-based.[7]

The heating of the planet is reason enough to change, but animal agriculture has many other devastating impacts on the world around us. Because it requires so much land, animal farming is a major driver of deforestation. Trees are cut down in order to make more space for animals to graze, or to grow the soy that is then shipped around the world to be fed to animals trapped inside factory farms. With the trees gone, climate change is exacerbated, and wildlife is lost.

In 2018, a major report from 59 leading scientists around the world concluded that we had lost 60 per cent of wild animal populations since 1970. The Living Planet Index found that the largest loss of wildlife was due to the destruction of natural habitats, much of it to create farmland for animal agriculture. The second largest cause was the killing of wild animals for human consumption, and that includes the trillions of fish taken from the oceans each year. In 2022, the outcome was even more bleak. The updated report concluded that around 70 per cent of wild animal populations have been lost since 1970.[8]

Not only does rearing animals for food require a lot more land, water and energy than producing plant-based foods, but it also produces a lot more pollutants. All those 70 billion animals must poop, and that waste has got to go somewhere. Too often it ends up in rivers, lakes and oceans, polluting the waters, killing off wildlife and creating toxic dead zones.

No wonder more and more people are embracing a more sustainable, lower-impact, wildlife-friendly, plant-based diet.

For Health

'Health' is such a broad term that it encompasses people who are searching for that famous 'vegan glow' as well as those who want to protect humanity from the next pandemic.

It's true that many, although not all, new vegans experience positive health changes, such as increased energy, better sleep, clearer skin and more comfortable digestion. But it is over the longer term that eating a plant-based vegan diet can really work its wonders. Eating a balanced vegan diet that prioritises whole natural foods has been associated with a reduced risk of many chronic diseases, including cardiovascular disease, type 2 diabetes and even some cancers.[9] Since these are among our biggest killers, it is no wonder that many people are eating more plants in order to reap the benefits both now and in the future.

And yet the impacts are bigger still. You may have read about antibiotic-resistant superbugs that can cause serious ill-health and even death. The reason such pathogens are on the rise is that we are misusing antibiotics, and that means these bugs are able to flourish. In order to preserve our life-saving drugs, we need to use them only when they are really needed. Yet the largest proportion of antibiotics is not dispensed by doctors and pharmacists; it is used inside factory farms in a bid to try and prevent animals from succumbing to disease amid the shocking conditions often found there.

A second humanitarian threat is from a global pandemic. We have already had a taste of what a zoonotic pathogen (one that comes from animals) can do, but there are viruses currently circulating inside chicken farms that have a higher mortality rate than Covid-19.[10] To date, thankfully, the existing bird and swine flu viruses have not found a way to spread easily among people, but that can change, and public health scientists are warning about the risks of keeping animals in conditions that are the perfect breeding ground for dangerous pathogens.

For the Good of All

Whatever reason has led you to eat more plants is a good one. Whether you want clearer skin, a liveable planet, an end to animal suffering or to live a long and healthy life, the benefits are not restricted to your one key motivation. You may get that beautiful skin, but you will also be reducing your climate impact, protecting the Earth's wild places, using fewer resources, reducing deforestation, encouraging wildlife to thrive, and protecting animals from harm. That's a pretty good result, all from eating tasty food!

GETTING STARTED

Whether you wish to include a few more plant-based meals in your diet or aim to become fully vegan, no one is going to go through your refrigerator or track your meals in a spreadsheet to see if you have stuck to your goal. This is your journey alone, and how you approach it is down to you. Some people find that gradually reducing the amount of meat, milk and eggs they eat is a sustainable way to make lasting change. They may start by being vegan before 6 p.m. or choose two fully vegan days a week. They may switch one product at a time, starting with a plant milk instead of dairy, before moving on to find the best vegan sausage, ice cream or pizza. Others may prefer to go 'cold turkey', clear out the cupboards, and head out to the supermarket for their first intrepid shopping trip as a vegan. Whatever route feels right to you is right, but please don't feel you have to make this journey alone.

First, Veganuary is here to help guide and support you, and to cheer you on. Millions of people have already taken part in our free month-long Try Vegan challenge. Sign up at Veganuary.com and you will receive daily emails for a month that give tips, ideas, recipes and inspiration. You can sign up any time of year, but most people take part in January. If you do, too, you will be part of an exciting global community of people all making the same positive changes as you – and going through the same challenges – all at the same time!

Beyond Veganuary, there is a wider community of vegans that you can connect with online. There are lots of vegan groups dedicated to food – from baking, to finding 'accidentally vegan' products, to eating out. You'll also find activist groups, vegan runners, vegan knitters, groups for vegan parenting and so much more. So, even if you are the only vegan you know, you will never be alone.

However, you don't need to confine your veganism to the digital world! There are also vegan meetups and events in towns and cities across the country. You'll find vegan fairs and festivals, conferences and trade events, and many chances to listen to speakers and connect with like-minded people. And you can bring it closer to home by inviting friends and family over to enjoy your new vegan signature dish or invite them to join you in a vegan cooking challenge. However you approach it, we hope this book will help you. Dip into it for inspiration, use it as a reference, or systematically work your way through all the recipes that sound tasty to you. There are no rules and no vegan police! This is your journey, so do it your way.

OUR TOP TEN TIPS

1 Sign up to take part in Veganuary. It's free, it's fun, and it exists to support you. Millions of people from almost every country on Earth have taken the Veganuary challenge, and 99 per cent say they would recommend it to a friend!

2 Find your why. Changing how we eat becomes a much smoother process when we know why we are making these changes. Spend some time to really understand why eating plant-based is such a positive step.

3 Check your cupboards. You may be surprised at how much vegan food is already in there! It's actually very common.

4 Do some research. If there are any foods you think you'll miss, find out if a vegan version exists (it probably does) or if you can make it yourself.

5 Make a meal plan. This can guide your next shopping trip as well as reassure you that you have plenty of tasty meals coming your way.

6 Veganise the meals you love. Many new vegans worry that they won't be able to enjoy a particular meal again, but the truth is most meals can be veganised quite simply.

7 Get creative. When you're ready, start branching out, trying ingredients, dishes and cuisines you haven't tried before. There is a wealth of options, so embrace the adventure.

8 Join a community. Whether you are a biker, hiker, metalhead or biscuit-lover, your vegan tribe exists and is waiting for you.

9 Enjoy eating out. Every high street caters for vegans now, and there is more choice than you might think, from chain restaurants to high-end, and from pubs to world cuisines.

10 Cut yourself some slack. Sometimes we may eat something accidentally, other times the temptation – or the hunger pangs – are just too strong to resist. It's OK. You're human. Just chalk it up to experience and move on.

STORE CUPBOARD SHOPPING LIST

So you're about to head out for your first plant-based shopping expedition and are looking to stock your cupboards with vegan essentials. This is what we recommend:

Vegetables

- Root vegetables, such as potatoes, sweet potatoes, parsnips, carrots
- Salad vegetables, including leaves, cucumbers, avocados, tomatoes, cress
- Frozen vegetables, like peas, sweetcorn, green beans, broad beans
- Leafy greens, such as broccoli, cabbage, kale, sprouts, spinach

Fruits

- 'Everyday' fruits, like bananas, apples, pears
- Cherries and berries, including raspberries, blueberries, strawberries (fresh or frozen)
- Citrus fruits, such as oranges, lemons, limes

Carbohydrates

- Bread, including sliced, ciabatta, rolls, bagels, fruit loaf, crumpets
- Pasta, such as spaghetti, fusilli, macaroni, lasagne
- Grains, like white, brown or wild rice, or quinoa, buckwheat, couscous

Protein

- Tofu, tempeh, seitan
- Vegan burgers, mince and sausages
- Beans, such as kidney, butter beans, borlotti, cannellini, baked beans
- Lentils, including green, brown, red (dried or tinned)
- Nuts and seeds, such as walnuts, hazelnuts, peanuts, sunflower seeds

Dairy Replacements

- Vegan butter, cheese, milk, yoghurt, cream, ice cream

Store Cupboard Staples

- Accompaniments, such as gravy granules, ketchup, sriracha, wholegrain mustard, vegan mayonnaise
- Tins, such as coconut milk, soups, tomatoes
- Breakfast foods like cereals, oatmeal
- Spreads such as peanut butter, yeast extract, jam, marmalade, hummus
- Spices including chilli powder, cumin, curry powder, smoked paprika
- Oils and vinegars, such as olive, sunflower and coconut oils, and balsamic or brown malt vinegar

Drinks

- Tea, herbal tea, coffee, fruit juice

Snacks

- Savoury foods like salted nuts, crisps, pretzels, crackers
- Sweet foods like chocolate, biscuits, doughnuts, cheesecakes

ONE-WEEK SAMPLE MEAL PLAN

There are so many vegan meals available to us, and yet new vegans understandably wonder what they are going to eat three times a day!

Mon	Tue	Wed	Thu
Breakfast: Toast and peanut butter or jam, with fruit juice	**Breakfast:** Porridge with seeds, and a cup of herbal tea	**Breakfast:** Bagel and vegan cream cheese, with apple juice	**Breakfast:** Mixed fresh fruits with chopped nuts and seeds
Lunch: Jacket potato with baked beans and salad	**Lunch:** Veggie and bean soup	**Lunch:** Spiced Chickpea Salad (page 149)	**Lunch:** Falafel wrap with hummus and salad
Dinner: Red Dragon Pie (page 64) with green veggies	**Dinner:** Veggie sausages, with potatoes, peas and gravy	**Dinner:** Mushroom Bolognese (page 82)	**Dinner:** One-pot Store Cupboard Curry (page 113)

Fri

Breakfast:
Sweet Spiced Apple
Pancakes (page 42)

Lunch:
Vegan sushi

Dinner:
Satay Traybake with
Smoked Tofu & Spicy
Sambal (page 70)

Sat

Breakfast:
Creamy Herbed
Mushrooms on Toast
(page 51)

Lunch:
Coronation Chickpea
Sandwich (page 120)

Dinner:
Smoky Mediterranean
Mac & Cheese (page
73)

Sun

Breakfast:
Baked Berry Oatmeal
with Caramelised
Walnuts (page 46)

Lunch:
Quiche (page 87) with
bean salad

Dinner:
Mushroom & Walnut
Wellington (page 79)
with roast potatoes
and fresh vegetables

GO-TO INGREDIENTS & NO-WASTE INSPIRATION

This is our little ingredients library to give you a helping hand if you want to stock up your store cupboard or get to grips with how to use different ingredients. None of these are hard to come by or difficult to cook with, and you might be surprised by how versatile everyday staples can be when you know how to use them! We've also included our 'no-waste inspiration' notes with simple advice on what to do with open or leftover ingredients, cross referencing to our lovely recipes, to ensure nothing goes to waste.

Agave

A syrup refined from the sap of the agave plant, which comes in dark and light varieties. Supermarkets stock it alongside their syrups and sugars.

No-waste inspiration: *Drizzle over ice cream; use in dressings and marinades; use as a sweetener for cakes; use in place of honey in warm drinks.* Try our Cowboy Caviar (page 136), Peanut Butter Breakfast Sundaes (page 54) or Sweet Spiced Apple Pancakes (page 42).

Ale

Not all beers are vegan, and not all companies label which ones are. However, most supermarkets allow you to filter your online searches to include only vegan items, so you can make a list of the ones you want before going to the store. Porter is a dark ale that can be substituted for stout. Check the supermarket website, the side of the bottle, or Barnivore.com to ensure your ale is vegan.

Almond butter

Found in most supermarkets and health food shops alongside the peanut butter.

Applesauce

Often comes in jars and is usually found with the condiments in supermarkets. It is a great replacement for eggs in cakes and pancakes.

No-waste inspiration: *Serve with porridge or breakfast cereals; mix into cake or cookie dough; add to snack bars or flapjacks; delicious on pancakes.*

Aquafaba

The liquid in a tin of chickpeas. It needs to be sieved to make sure any particles are removed before using in desserts. Alternatively, you can buy cartons of ready-to-use aquafaba online and in health food shops.

No-waste inspiration: *Gives lightness to baked goods, so add to pancakes, muffins, cakes and cookies.*

Try our Nutty Choc Chip Cookies (page 202), Bakewell Tart (page 208) or Raspberry & Rose Pistachio Pavlova (page 190).

Bacon, vegan

Readily available in supermarket freezer and refrigerator sections. Most vegetarian bacon is vegan, but not all, so check the pack.

No-waste inspiration: *Make BLT sandwiches; add to pasta sauces; include in a full English breakfast; add to pizza.*

Try our Creamy Carbonara with Coconut Bacon (page 60).

Barbecue sauce/seasoning

There are lots of varieties of barbecue sauce around, and most are vegan. Barbecue seasoning is a blend of herbs and spices, dried and ground, which can be found in supermarkets in the spice aisle.

Basil

Fresh

This Italian herb is readily available, but if you can't find it, just omit it from the recipe, as in most of our recipes it can't be replaced by dried basil.

Thai

A fresh herb found in some supermarkets. If it's not available, you can use the usual Italian basil, which is more commonly available.

No-waste inspiration: *Add to salads; use in Thai recipes, such as coconut curries and satays.*

Bay leaves

Dried leaves found in supermarkets in the spice aisle; these are left in dishes for their flavour during cooking but should be removed before serving.

Beans

Aduki

A small red-brown bean commonly available tinned in supermarkets. If they're not available, try black beans or black-eyed beans.

Black

Also known as turtle beans, these are not the same as black-eyed beans. Black beans can be bought tinned or dried. The dried beans take an hour to cook, whereas the tinned beans can be used immediately.

No-waste inspiration: *Delicious in bean salads, as a base for chilli non carne, or in burritos.*
Try our Black Bean Mole with Sweet Potato Fries (page 74) or Cowboy Caviar (page 136).
Butter
A large white bean with a smooth creamy texture. You'll find them tinned in supermarkets.
No-waste inspiration: *Add to bean chillies and casseroles; make a butter bean dip; add to spicy tomato sauce; add to salads.*
Try our One-pot Butter Bean & Root Veg Stew with Cheesy Dumplings (page 108).
Cannellini
These can be bought dried or tinned in most supermarkets. The dried ones are cheaper but will need to be soaked overnight before use.
Kidney
A dark red bean, shaped like a kidney, that is commonly used in chilli non carne.
No-waste inspiration: *Add to bean salads and chilli non carne; make tasty bean burgers.*
Try our Souperfood Soup (page 170), BeaNut Burger (page 62) or Every Day Dal (page 107).

Black treacle

A mixture of cane molasses and syrup, with a rich strong flavour, this is a surprisingly useful source of calcium. Find it in supermarkets in the baking aisle.
No-waste inspiration: *Use in baked goods such as gingerbread, flapjacks and parkin.*
Try our Peanut Butter Flapjacks (page 213), Porridge Bread (page 174) or Strawberry Gingerbread Breakfast Pots (page 44).

Breadcrumbs

You can buy breadcrumbs, but it is a whole lot cheaper to make your own by taking bread (either fresh or a few days old) and blitzing it in a food processor.
No-waste inspiration: *Make a gratin topping; use in stuffing; use to thicken sauces or hold together ingredients in a pie.*
Try our Roast Red Pepper & Walnut Dip (page 152) or Treacle Tart (page 191).

Buckwheat (toasted)

Eaten as a grain but actually a fruit, so it can be eaten by those who can't tolerate gluten. Find it with the rice and other grains in the supermarket, or sometimes in the world foods section.
No-waste inspiration: *Use instead of rice to accompany a main meal; add to burritos; try using it to make porridge.*

Butter, vegan

All supermarkets stock more than one type of vegan butter, and you'll find them in the refrigerator alongside the dairy versions. Some are made from sunflower oil, others from soya, olive oil or avocado.

Cacao powder

This is the milled cocoa bean, which is said to have better health benefits than cocoa powder. It is readily available in supermarkets, often in the whole foods section, but if you can't find it, use cocoa powder instead.

Capers

These small, intensely flavoured buds from a Mediterranean bush can single-handedly perk up a tomato sauce. Also delicious on pizzas. Find them in jars alongside the pickles in the supermarket.
No-waste inspiration: *Add to pasta or potato salad; use as a pizza topping; add to spaghetti sauce or aubergine parmigiana.*
Try our Zesty Olive Tapenade (page 154), One-Pot Mediterranean Linguine (page 86) or Beetroot & Fennel with Orange Wild Rice (page 144).

Caraway seeds

These little seeds (which are actually fruits) have a distinctive flavour and are often used in baking. Find them in the spice aisle of the supermarket.

Cardamom pods

The seed pod of the cardamom plant, these can be found in the spice aisle. They add flavour to curries, rice dishes and spiced drinks.

Cayenne

A powdered medium-hot chilli pepper found in the spice aisle.

Celery salt

This is a mix of sea salt and celery powder and can be found in the spice aisle.

Cheese, vegan

All supermarkets stock non-dairy cheeses in a variety of flavours and styles, including Cheddar-style and Greek-style (feta). You'll find them in the supermarket refrigerator section, often in a designated 'free from' area, away from the dairy cheeses. Watch out for 'lactose-free' cheese, which still contains dairy.
Cream cheese
Many supermarkets stock vegan cream cheese. in various flavours. It is great for sandwiches and dips, while the natural (plain) flavour can also be used in cheesecakes and frosting.
No-waste inspiration: *Eat in sandwiches with salad and herbs; use in creamy pasta sauces; make a dip for crackers and raw veggies.*
Try our Chocolate Orange Oreo Cheesecake (page 182) or Veggie Wraps (page 130).

Feta

A creamy white Greek cheese that now comes in a vegan version. It is commonly available in supermarkets and online.

No-waste inspiration: *Make a Greek salad; add to grain-based salads; stir into pasta sauces; add to pies.*

Try our Walnut, Rosemary & Feta Rolls (page 122).

Parmesan

Many supermarkets stock this alongside other vegan cheeses, and you can find it easily online. Alternatively, it's fine to use another vegan hard cheese instead.

No-waste inspiration: *Grate over pasta dishes or risotto; add to pasta bakes; add to mashed potatoes as a side dish or on top of a shepherd's pie.*

Chia seeds

A very useful seed, often found in the whole food section of the supermarket and in health food shops. It is highly nutritious and, when soaked in water, can be used in place of eggs in baking.

No-waste inspiration: *Add to smoothies; mix into salad dressings; sprinkle on breakfasts; add to pancakes or baked goods.*

Chickpeas

These can be bought tinned or dried. The dried ones are cheaper, but they need to be soaked overnight and simmered for an hour or more, so the tinned ones are more convenient. Plus, they come with free aquafaba (see page 22)!

No-waste inspiration: *Add to vegetable soups and stews; make a bean salad; make hummus.*

Try our Chickpea 'Tuna' Melt (page 116), Spiced Chickpea Salad (page 149), or Breakfast Burrito with Sriracha Mayo (page 56).

Chilli flakes

Found in the spice aisle. Some supermarkets carry different types, including Kashmiri and chipotle, but you can use any dried flakes you find. Some, like ancho, are milder and you may wish to add more of them.

Chillies, fresh

Found in the produce section of the supermarket.

Green

In these recipes we are referring to the larger green chillies. Green finger chillies (see page 26) are much hotter, so if you use those, you may wish to reduce the quantity (or, you may not!).

No-waste inspiration: *Spice up curries and chilli non carne; lovely in guacamole, burritos and stir-fries.*

Try our Hearts of Palm Ceviche (page 138) or Cowboy Caviar (page 136).

Chives

These fresh herbs, which have a slight oniony flavour, are readily available in the produce section of the supermarket, but are also very easy to grow in a garden, window box or on a shelf in the kitchen.

No-waste inspiration: *Add to salads; sprinkle on soups and risottos; add to mashed or baked potatoes; add to creamy dips or savoury scones.* Try our Creamy Herbed Mushrooms on Toast (page 51).

Chocolate

There are many vegan 'milk' chocolates available, including in supermarkets where they are often in the 'free from' section. Many dark chocolates are vegan. Don't worry if it says 'cocoa butter' in the ingredients – it is not made with dairy.

No-waste inspiration: *Eat dark chocolate; melt it over ice cream; grate over cakes or desserts; melt and dip fruits or biscuits into it.* Try our Easy Vegan Chocolate Cake (page 210), Chocolate Orange Oreo Cheesecake (page 182) or Rocky Road Fridge Cake (page 199).

Chocolate chips

Little pieces of chocolate that are perfect for cookies. Some supermarkets stock vegan versions, or you can break up dark, dairy-free buttons, or roughly chop up a dark vegan chocolate bar.

No-waste inspiration: *Add to cakes and cookies.* Try our Cherry Chocolate Rock Cakes (page 219) or Choc Chip Banana Bread (page 212).

Red

In these recipes we are referring to the larger red chillies. If you like more heat, try bird's-eye chillies.

No-waste inspiration: *Use in curries and chilli non carne; add to salsas and spicy soups.* Try our Sweetcorn Fritters with Sweet Chilli Sauce (page 126).

Finger

These are smaller and slimmer than standard chillies, but they are also significantly hotter.

No-waste inspiration: *Add some heat to chilli non carne, Thai curries and Mexican or Indian dishes.* Try our Hearts of Palm Ceviche (page 138) or Cowboy Caviar (page 136).

Chorizo, vegan

There is a vegan version of just about everything, including this popular spiced sausage. Look in the freezer and refrigerator sections of the supermarket, but if you can't find it, just pick a different vegan sausage, or order it online.
No-waste inspiration: *Add to risottos, paellas, stews, pizzas or pasta sauce.*

Cinnamon

Can be bought ground or in sticks; our recipes only use ground cinnamon, which can be found in the spice aisle of the supermarket.

Cocoa

A powder made by crushing the beans of the cacao tree. It's readily available and is vegan (although some of the hot chocolate powders that are made using it may not be).

Coconut

Creamed
Solid coconut, pressed into a block. You'll find it on the shelves of all supermarkets, often in the world foods section.

Desiccated
Dried flakes of coconut which are available in supermarkets, usually in the baking aisle.
No-waste inspiration: *Sprinkle over breakfast cereal; sprinkle over curries before serving; add to brownies, cookies and macaroons.*

Try our Pasta Frola – Quince Tart (page 196), Rocky Road Fridge Cake (page 199) or Coconut Rum Chocolate Pots with a Spike of Chilli (page 188).

Flakes
Also sold as flaked coconut, these are not always available in supermarkets but can often be found in health food shops and online.
No-waste inspiration: *Add to breakfast cereal or porridge; make granola; sprinkle over cakes or make coconut cookies.*

Milk
Tinned coconut milk can usually be found in the world foods section of the supermarket. You'll find lower-fat varieties if you prefer them.
No-waste inspiration: *Serve over ice; make cocktails; add a splash to fruit salads and compotes; add to baked goods.*

Oil
This solid oil is usually stocked with the other oils, but it may also be in the whole food section of the supermarket. It is not the same as creamed coconut or coconut cream, and those won't work as a substitute. If you can't find coconut oil, use another vegetable oil such as sunflower or rapeseed.

Coriander

Fresh leaf coriander can be found in supermarkets alongside other fresh herbs; ground coriander (made from the seeds) will be in the spice aisle. If you are unlucky enough to have the gene that makes coriander leaves taste like soap, just omit it from any recipe.

No-waste inspiration: *Sprinkle on soups or curries; add to salads; delicious in guacamole and burritos.*
Try our Rainbow Pineapple Salad (page 148), Coronation Chickpea Sandwich (page 120), Sweetcorn Fritters with Sweet Chilli Sauce (page 126), Thai Green Curry (page 66) or Chickpea Chole Chawal with Raita (page 100).

Cream, vegan

Oat or soy

This is a single cream substitute that can be found in supermarkets. It comes in a carton and may be either in the refrigerator or on the shelf with the long-life milks.

No-waste inspiration: *Stir into soups and curries; use as a base for creamy sauces; eat with cakes and desserts.*
Try our Creamy Herbed Mushrooms on Toast (page 51) or Sticky Toffee Pudding (page 185).

Whippable

There are now whippable vegan creams available. Find them in the refrigerator section of the supermarket and online. Don't try to whip single or double vegan creams, as they just won't work.

No-waste inspiration: *Eat with fruit or on scones; serve with sticky toffee pudding, hot chocolate puddings or your favourite dessert.*
Try our Banoffee Pie (page 180) or Raspberry & Rose Pistachio Pavlova (page 190).

Cumin

This can be bought as seeds or ground into a powder. In our recipes, we are referring to ground cumin unless stated otherwise.

Curry powder

There are mild, medium and hot curry powders, so choose the one that suits you best.

Dill

Found with other fresh herbs, but if you can't find fresh dill, use the dried version and use one-third of the amount.

No-waste inspiration: *Use in potato salads, soups and creamy dips.*
Try our Buffalo Wings with Creamy Dill Dip (page 124), Creamy Herbed Mushrooms on Toast (page 51) or Beetroot & Fennel with Orange Wild Rice (page 144).

Fenugreek leaves

Also known as methi, these dried leaves are commonly used in Indian cookery. Find them in the spice aisle or in the world foods section of the supermarket.

Flax seed, ground

This can be found in either the baking section or the whole foods section of most supermarkets. When soaked in water, it creates an 'egg' which can be used in baking.

No-waste inspiration: *Sprinkle on breakfast cereal or porridge; use as an egg replacement in baking.* Try our Lemon Crêpes (page 198), Cherry Chocolate Rock Cakes (page 219) or Porter Cake (page 218).

Garam masala

A blend of different spices used in Indian cuisine, each brand is slightly different. Find it in the spice aisle.

Ginger

Ground
Powdered ginger root, found in the spice aisle.
Fresh
A knobbly root that is found in the fresh produce aisle.

No-waste inspiration: *Grate and add to curries and stir-fries; slice into herbal teas; add the juice to smoothies and juices; make gingerbread.* Try our Cambodian Samlá-Style Curry (page 84), Every Day Dal (page 107), Sticky Ginger Sesame Tofu (page 106), Ramen (page 162) or Pumpkin Thai-Spiced Soup (page 168).

Hearts of palm

Pale spears from the palm tree. Found tinned in many supermarkets and can be ordered online.

Hoisin

A thick, tangy, sweet sauce made with fermented soya beans, found in most supermarkets. It is almost always vegan.

Hot pepper sauce

There are many brands of hot sauce available on the market and most are vegan. They can usually be found in supermarkets with the condiments and other sauces. See also **Sriracha**, below.

Jackfruit

This is indeed a fruit; meaty in texture and able to take on the flavours it is cooked with. It is available tinned in most supermarkets, in the world foods section or the tinned goods aisle. Try our Barbecued Pulled Jackfruit Sandwich with Slaw (page 92)

Jam

Almost all jams are vegan, as they tend to be made from just sugar, fruit and pectin, a gelling agent made from fruit.

Kala namak

Also known as black salt, this has an eggy flavour due to its high sulphur content. It is not available in all supermarkets, so you may need to order it online, though it is optional in our recipes.

Lemongrass/lemongrass purée

You can find fresh lemongrass in the produce section of many supermarkets, but the purée may be easier to find, store and use. You'll usually find it in the world foods section.
No-waste inspiration: *Use in Thai recipes such as soups and coconut curries.*
Try our Pumpkin Thai-Spiced Soup (page 168), Thai Green Curry (page 66) or Cambodian Samlá-style Curry (page 84).

Lentils

Green

Slightly larger than red lentils, these are great when you want more texture. Tinned lentils are the most convenient, but you can also buy dried lentils, which are cheaper but take about 40 minutes to cook.
No-waste inspiration: *Add to stews and casseroles; make a green lentil dal or a tasty filling soup.*
Try our Argentinian Shepherd's Pie (page 99).

Puy

These are brown lentils with a slightly peppery flavour that hold their texture well. You can buy them pre-cooked in pouches in supermarkets, or you can substitute them with tinned brown lentils.
No-waste inspiration: *Add to soups, salads and curries, or stir into pasta sauces.*

Red

These are small, dried lentils that need no pre-soaking. They are nutritious and very tasty, so don't believe the hippy hype! Check the pack, as they may be whole red lentils or they may be split red lentils, which take less time to cook.
No-waste inspiration: *Add to stews and soups to thicken; make a dal.*
Try our One-Pot Mediterranean Linguine (page 86), Souperfood Soup (page 170) or Every Day Dal (page 107).

Liquid smoke

A natural product made from condensing wood smoke. It's not on all supermarket shelves, but can be ordered online. If it's not available, just leave it out of the recipe.

No-waste inspiration: *Add a drop or two to any savoury dish where you like a smoky flavour, such as burgers and hotdogs, to get that barbecue taste; add to marinades, sauces and dips.*
Add a little to our Kedgeree with Herby Yoghurt (page 52) or try our Creamy Carbonara with Coconut Bacon (page 60).

Maple syrup

Available in supermarkets but it can be expensive, so substitute with golden syrup or agave syrup.

Meat substitutes

Beef-style pieces, vegan
There are several varieties available, some in supermarket freezer sections, others refrigerated. If you can't get them locally, look in your nearest health food shop or online.

Soya mince, frozen
Most supermarkets stock either their own brand or a branded version of this low-fat, high-protein, plant-based mince. The frozen version gives a better texture than the dried, but dried is cheaper and can be substituted in our recipes if preferred.

Sausages, vegan
There are many vegan sausages available in supermarkets. Check the freezer and refrigerated sections for different types.

Milk, vegan

All supermarkets stock a variety of plant milks including oat, soya, almond, cashew and coconut. You may also find rice, hemp, hazelnut and others. If the recipe does not specify, use whichever one you have or like best. If it does specify and you prefer another, the recipe will still work fine.

Mint

You can buy packets of fresh mint in the supermarket, but if they have it growing in pots, buy one of those and keep it on a windowsill for a regular supply of zingy leaves.

No-waste inspiration: *Add to leafy salads; lovely in savoury rice or couscous dishes; make mint tea; add to cold drinks.*
Try our Minted Pea Hummus (page 158), Gochujang Roasted Cauliflower with Herbed Quinoa & Mint Mayo Drizzle (page 67), Spiced Chickpea Salad (page 149), Souperfood Soup (page 170), Chickpea Chole Chawal with Raita (page 100) or Strawberry Gingerbread Breakfast Pots (page 44).

Miso paste

A fermented savoury paste, made from soybeans, found in jars on the shelves, and sometimes in tubs in the refrigerator section of the supermarket. White miso has a lighter flavour than brown or red, but choose whichever one you prefer.

No-waste inspiration: *Use in soups and broths, marinades and dressings – anywhere you want a lovely savoury umami flavour.*
Try our Ramen (page 162) or Smoky Mediterranean Mac & Cheese (page 73).

Molasses

There are various types, but you may have to visit a health food shop to buy them. For convenience, you can use black treacle, which is stocked in supermarkets.

Mushrooms, dried

Porcini
These can be bought in tubs in supermarkets. They need to be rehydrated before use, and they give a rich, umami flavour to savoury dishes.
Shiitake
These can also be bought in tubs in supermarkets. They need to be rehydrated before use and give an intense, earthy flavour to savoury dishes.

Mustard, Dijon, English or wholegrain

Most shop-bought mustards are made with spirit vinegar, which means they are vegan. Most supermarket websites state which ones are vegan, and many of the labels will also make it clear.

No-waste inspiration: *Serve Dijon mustard as an accompaniment to nut roasts or with burgers or hot dogs; use in salad dressings; add to savoury creamy sauces or to mayonnaise.*
Try English mustard instead of wholegrain or Dijon in our Creamy Herbed Mushrooms on Toast (page 51) or Brazilian Aubergine Stroganoff (page 102).

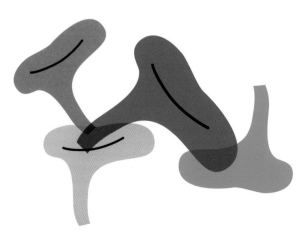

Nori

This is a seaweed, often sold in sheets in the world foods section of the supermarket. It gives a lovely taste-of-the-sea flavour to dishes.
No-waste inspiration: *Add to miso soups; sprinkle on noodle salads; add to rice dishes such as sushi.*

Nutmeg

Found in the spice aisle of the supermarket, this usually comes as a whole seed. You'll need to grate it to get the required amount.

Nutritional yeast

A powder or flake that has a lovely cheesy taste and is rich in most of the B vitamins. Some supermarkets stock it in the 'free from' section, otherwise it can be bought online or from health food shops.
No-waste inspiration: *Sprinkle over pasta sauces; add to cheese sauces and cheesy dishes; great in savoury scones and pancakes.*
Try our Smoky Mediterranean Mac & Cheese (page 73) or Grilled Caesar Salad (page 134).

Orange extract

Found in the baking aisle of the supermarket in tiny bottles alongside the vanilla extract and other cake flavourings.
No-waste inspiration: *Add to cakes, cheesecakes and pancakes when you want that orangey zing.*

Oregano, dried

Found in the spice section of the supermarket. Great for Italian and Mexican dishes.

Paprika

Found in the spice aisle, and not to be confused with smoked paprika, which has a distinctive smoky flavour. You'll find them both in the spice section of the supermarket.

Parsley

Curled or flat-leaf, use whichever you can find or prefer. It can be found with other fresh herbs in the produce section of the supermarket.
No-waste inspiration: *Sprinkle over salads, soups, savoury tarts and rice dishes; add to coleslaw, flans and pasta sauces.*
Try our Buckwheat Tabbouleh (page 140), German Potato Salad (page 142) or Buffalo Wings with Creamy Dill Dip (page 124).

Passata

A thick liquid made by cooking and straining tomatoes so that there are no lumps of tomato left. It is found in all supermarkets, usually in cartons or jars near the tinned tomatoes. If you can't find it, blend tinned tomatoes instead.
No-waste inspiration: *Use wherever you would use tinned tomatoes; add to soups, stews, curries and casseroles; use as a pizza base.*
Try our One-Pot Mediterranean Linguine (page 86).

Pastry, puff and shortcrust

Many commercial puff and shortcrust pastries are vegan, so check the ingredients of both the branded version and the supermarket's own. Found in the refrigerated section.
No-waste inspiration: *Use pastry offcuts to make mini jam tarts, or spread with pesto and bake to make savoury tartlets.*

Peppercorns

The whole dried fruit, commonly ground as a seasoning; found in the spice aisle.

Pomegranate molasses

A common ingredient in Middle Eastern cooking, this can be found in the world foods section of many supermarkets. It is optional in our dishes, so just leave it out if you can't find it.
No-waste inspiration: *Add to roast vegetables; use in marinades and dressings; stir into hummus or cake frosting.*

Quinoa

Seeds that are cooked and eaten like grains. Quinoa (pronounced keen-wa) is a complete source of protein, very tasty, and can be used in place of rice. It is available in supermarkets and will be found either alongside the rice or in the whole foods section.

Ramen noodles

Most supermarkets stock these wheat-based noodles and most are vegan. They can usually be found in the world foods section.
No-waste inspiration: *Serve with stir-fries or coconut-based curries; add to Thai soups.*

Ras el hanout

A spice blend used in North African cookery that typically contains coriander, black pepper, cinnamon and allspice as well as other spices. Found in the spice aisle.

Rice noodles

Most supermarkets stock rice noodles, which can usually be found in the world foods section. They rehydrate almost instantly, so are great for a quick meal.
No-waste inspiration: *Serve with stir-fries or coconut-based curries; add to Thai soups.*

Rosemary

Available fresh or dried. If using fresh, you'll need two or three times the quantity of dried.
No-waste inspiration: *Add to roast potatoes or other roasted vegetables; add to mac & cheese; lovely with veggie skewers; make flavoured olive oil.*
Try our Celeriac Soup with Garlic Croutons (page 166), Sausage & New Potato Traybake (page 78) or Mushroom & Walnut Wellington (page 79).

Rose petals

A pretty garnish for salads and sweet dishes. All rose petals are edible, so pick your own or buy them online and in some supermarkets.

Rose water

A liquid made by steeping rose petals in water to give it a gentle flavour. Used in Middle Eastern, Indian and Chinese cuisines, it can be found in the baking aisle of the supermarket, in health food shops and online.
No-waste inspiration: *Add to cake frosting, muffin mixes and sorbets; mix with fruit syrups for pouring over ice cream and pancakes.*

Rum

Dark
Almost every dark rum is vegan. You can check on Barnivore.com.
Coconut
There are many brands of coconut rum that are vegan. Check on Barnivore.com or look at the maker's website.
No-waste inspiration: *Serve it over ice; make cocktails; add a splash to fruit salads and compotes; add to baked goods.*

Salt

Use table salt, sea salt, Himalayan pink salt or iodised salt. They all do the same thing.

Sesame

Seeds
These are readily available in supermarkets, either in the baking aisle or in the whole foods section. They're usually plain, but they can sometimes be found already toasted, which intensifies their flavour.
No-waste inspiration: *Sprinkle over salads, soups and stir-fries; add to bread; add to porridge and breakfast cereals.*
Try our Sticky Ginger Sesame Tofu (page 106).
Oil
Sometimes called toasted sesame oil, this is a rich, flavourful oil used in many Asian dishes. It is readily available in supermarkets alongside the other oils.
No-waste inspiration: *Add to stir-fries at the end for that uniquely delicious flavour.*
Try our Ramen (page 162) or Sticky Ginger Sesame Tofu (page 106).

Sriracha sauce

A Thai hot pepper sauce that is readily available; it's fine to substitute other hot sauces if you can't get hold of sriracha. See **hot pepper sauce**, page 30.
No-waste inspiration: *Add to any dish where you'd like a little heat, such as chilli non carne, Thai curries, burritos and spicy noodles.*
Try our Breakfast Burrito with Sriracha Mayo (page 56) or Argentinian Locro Stew (page 104).

Star anise

Possibly the prettiest spice, this can be used in a variety of dishes to add a liquorice flavour. Find it in the spice aisle.

Sugar, coconut

Found in many supermarkets alongside other sugars, but if it's not available, use a light brown sugar instead.

Tabasco sauce

A brand of red pepper sauce that is widely available in supermarkets and is naturally vegan.

Tahini

A creamy paste made from sesame seeds which is often used in hummus and on kebabs. It comes in jars and can be found in the world foods section of most supermarkets.
No-waste inspiration: *Make hummus; eat with falafel; add to dips and dressings; add to cakes and brownies.*
Try our Spiced Chickpea Salad (page 149), Citrus Summer Greens with Tahini Lime Drizzle (page 128) or Carrot Cake with Orange Frosting (page 216).

Tamari

Japanese soy sauce. Readily available in supermarkets, but you can use dark soy sauce instead.

Thai red curry paste

Many readily available brands of red curry paste are vegan. Just look out for those that contain anchovies or fish sauce.
No-waste inspiration: *As well as Thai red curries, use in soups, stews and salad dressings.*

Thyme, dried or fresh

Use half the quantity if using the dried herb. Both can be found in supermarkets, or you can grow a pot of thyme in your kitchen or garden.
No-waste inspiration: *Use in mushroom risotto, stuffings, savoury pies or bean stews.*
Try our 'Beef' & Ale Pie (page 95) or Mushroom & Walnut Wellington (page 79).

Tofu

Also known as beancurd, tofu is made from soya beans and is a high-protein staple of many Asian and vegan dishes. It doesn't taste of much on its own, but it soaks up flavours.

Firm

This is the regular tofu that you find in supermarkets. It is often set using calcium sulphate, which makes it a great source of calcium.

No-waste inspiration: *Marinate and stir-fry or bake; add to stews; cover with cornflour and fry for a crispy addition to stir-fries; add to curry sauces; blend to use in dips; barbecue as steaks or in veggie kebabs.*

Try our Sticky Ginger Sesame Tofu (page 106), Super Tofu & Veg Scramble on Toast (page 48) or Goulash with Mashed Potatoes (page 112).

Marinated

Many supermarkets stock tofu that has already been flavoured or marinated. Check the refrigerator section.

Silken

This has a smoother, silkier texture than regular tofu, which means it can be blended into a cream (for cheesecakes and sauces). It tends to be packed in shelf-stable cartons and you are likely to find it in the world foods section of the supermarket.

No-waste inspiration: *Make into a creamy sauce; douse in soy sauce and toasted sesame oil and add to a bento box; add to smoothies or pancakes.*

Smoked

As its name suggests, this has a smoky flavour, which means it does not need flavours to be added. It is available in most supermarkets and can be bought online.

No-waste inspiration: *Add to stir-fries; bake in coconut milk; slice for sandwiches.*

Try our Ramen (page 162), Satay Traybake with Smoked Tofu & Spicy Sambal (page 70) or Goulash with Mashed Potatoes (page 112).

Tomatoes

Sun-dried

Found in tubs or jars with the antipasti or pasta sauces, or in the deli section of the supermarket. Don't be put off if you see 'lactic acid' on the ingredient list – it does not come from milk.

No-waste inspiration: *Add to pasta sauces and bakes; add to lasagne and bolognese sauce; use as a pizza topping; add to salads.*

Try our One-Pot Mediterranean Linguine (page 86) or Veggie Wraps (page 130).

Sun-dried paste/purée

A rich, flavourful paste that can be found in supermarkets, often alongside the pasta sauces. Be careful not to confuse it with sun-dried tomato pesto, which is unlikely to be vegan.

Turmeric

A spice with proven health benefits, and a little goes a long way. Be careful! This bright yellow spice can stain.

Vanilla extract

Found in tiny bottles in the baking aisle. You can also use vanilla bean paste, or vanilla essence, which is an artificial vanilla flavouring.
No-waste inspiration: *Add to cakes, cookies, pancakes and desserts.*
Try our Emperor's Pancakes (page 194), Blueberry Muffins (page 206), Easy Vegan Chocolate Cake (page 210), Coconut Rum Chocolate Pots with a Spike of Chilli (page 188) or Sticky Toffee Pudding (page 185).

Wine

Some of the products used to clarify wines are not vegan. Some companies state on the bottle whether the wine is vegan; others don't. But you can usually filter your online supermarket searches to include only vegan items, which lets you make a list of the ones you want before going to the store. Alternatively, check Barnivore.com.

Worcestershire sauce

Traditional Worcestershire sauce contains fish, but there are vegan versions available (sometimes called Worcester sauce). You may need to order it online or look for it in a health food shop.
No-waste inspiration: *Add to tomato-based sauces such as in chilli non carne or root vegetable stews.*

Yoghurt, coconut

Available in most supermarkets. It has a distinctive flavour that is less sweet than other vegan yoghurts, which makes it perfect for pairing with savoury dishes, and for dressing with syrup and fruits.
No-waste inspiration: *Eat for breakfast with fruit, cereal or porridge; eat with pancakes; make a raita to go with curries.*
Try our Kedgeree with Herby Yoghurt (page 52), Roasted Pumpkin with Moroccan-Style Couscous & Coconut-Lime Yoghurt (page 90), Strawberry Gingerbread Breakfast Pots (page 44) or Baked Berry Oatmeal with Caramelised Walnuts (page 46).

1.

BREAKFAST

These American-style pancakes are always incredibly popular and the recipe couldn't be easier. In just a few minutes, you'll have a very tasty and filling breakfast, which means you don't have to wait for the weekend to try them. Eat them just as they are, or serve them with a drizzle of agave syrup and some fresh berries. They can also be rolled up for a portable breakfast if you are on the go.

SWEET SPICED APPLE PANCAKES

MAKES 6 PANCAKES

150g plain flour
2 teaspoons baking powder
½ teaspoon salt
½ teaspoon ground cinnamon
¼ teaspoon ground nutmeg
4 tablespoons applesauce
2 tablespoons agave syrup
200ml plant milk
a little light-flavoured oil, such as
    sunflower

TO SERVE
your choice of blueberries, strawberries, or raspberries, and some agave syrup

1. In a bowl, mix the flour, baking powder, salt, cinnamon and nutmeg, and combine well.
2. In a separate bowl, combine the applesauce, agave and plant milk. Stir into the flour mix.
3. Heat a lightly oiled frying pan over a medium-high heat and when it's hot, add a good half a ladle of the batter mix at a time. Cook until the bubbles on the surface of the pancake do not close when they pop, then turn the pancake over and cook until the underside is golden.
4. Serve straight away, with fresh berries and a drizzle of agave syrup.

These are so pretty and so appetising that you can enjoy them as a dessert, too. If you're eating this for breakfast, you may wish to make the granola and compote ahead of time, but you can always take the short cut if time is tight and assemble the pots from shop-bought versions instead. We won't tell anyone.

STRAWBERRY GINGERBREAD BREAKFAST POTS

SERVES 4

FOR THE GINGERBREAD GRANOLA
1 tablespoon sunflower oil or
    melted coconut oil
60ml maple syrup
1 tablespoon molasses or
    black treacle
½ teaspoon vanilla extract
150g rolled oats
125g mixed nuts, roughly
    chopped
1 teaspoon ground ginger
½ teaspoon ground cinnamon

FOR THE COMPOTE
250g strawberries, washed,
    hulled and halved (fresh or
    frozen and defrosted)
2 tablespoons caster sugar
½ orange, zest and juice
1 teaspoon cornflour

TO SERVE
300g coconut yoghurt
8 fresh strawberries, washed
    and halved
some fresh mint leaves

1. Make the gingerbread granola in advance. Heat the oven to 160°C fan/350°F/Gas Mark 4.
2. Mix the wet ingredients together in a large bowl, then add the dry ingredients and mix thoroughly.
3. Spread the mixture on a large baking tray and bake for 20 minutes, stirring it about halfway through the cooking time. Remove the tray from the oven and let the granola cool. It will crisp up as it does so.
4. To make the compote, put the strawberries, sugar and orange zest and juice into a pan and bring to the boil. Reduce the heat and simmer for 10 minutes.
5. In a small bowl, mix the cornflour into 3 teaspoons of water and stir it into the strawberries to thicken the sauce. Remove the compote from the heat and let it cool.
6. In your serving glasses or pots, layer the granola, yoghurt, compote and fresh fruit, and garnish with mint leaves.

How did such a simple idea get to be so delicious? You can adapt this recipe however you like so it's different every morning, but we always include peanut butter because, in our view, everything is improved with peanut butter. Make the oats the night before for a ready-to-go breakfast. It's also portable, so if you're running late, you can take it with you.

PEANUT BUTTER OVERNIGHT OATS

SERVES 1

150ml plant milk
2 tablespoons peanut butter
1 tablespoon syrup (golden, agave, or maple)
50g oats
1 tablespoon dried cranberries
1 teaspoon chia seeds
¼ teaspoon ground cinnamon

1. Warm the plant milk, peanut butter and syrup in the microwave or very gently in a pan until the peanut butter has melted into the milk.
2. Place the rest of the ingredients in a bowl or mason jar and mix well. Add the milk and peanut butter mixture and stir well.
3. Press down with a spoon to ensure all the oats are immersed in the milk.
4. Cover and refrigerate until morning to allow it to thicken up.
5. You can eat it as it is or heat it up in the microwave, and top with fresh sliced banana, blueberries, or anything else you like.

If you haven't tried baked oatmeal yet, you are missing out.
These nutritious oats are sweetened with agave and fruit,
and those super tasty caramelised walnuts. This may not be
the breakfast to make if you are rushing for the morning bus,
but if you make it ahead of time, it should last you through
the week.

BAKED BERRY OATMEAL WITH CARAMELISED WALNUTS

SERVES 4–6

175g oats
2 teaspoons ground cinnamon
¼ teaspoon ground nutmeg
1 teaspoon baking powder
½ teaspoon salt
325ml plant milk
70ml agave or maple syrup
4 tablespoons peanut butter
1 teaspoon vanilla extract
2 tablespoons coconut oil,
    melted
250g cherries or berries of your
    choice, fresh or frozen
55g walnut pieces
20g brown sugar
½ tablespoon vegan butter
coconut yoghurt, to serve

1. Heat the oven to 180°C fan/400°F/Gas Mark 6.
2. In a large bowl, combine the oats, cinnamon, nutmeg, baking
   powder and salt.
3. In a separate bowl, mix together the milk, syrup, peanut butter,
   vanilla extract and the melted coconut oil.
4. Put half the fruit in the bottom of an ovenproof dish (around
   20 x 20cm), cover it with the oat mixture, then pour over the wet
   mixture, ensuring all the oats get soaked.
5. Put the rest of the fruit on top and bake for 40 minutes, until the top
   is golden.
6. Meanwhile, heat a frying pan over a medium heat and add the
   walnuts, sugar and vegan butter. Keep stirring until the sugar has
   melted and the walnuts are coated – about 2–3 minutes. Set aside.
7. When the oats have 7–8 minutes left to cook, scatter the walnuts
   over the top and put the dish back into the oven to finish cooking.
8. Serve warm or cool, with some coconut yoghurt.

This is the kind of breakfast that will easily keep you fuelled all the way to lunch and beyond. High in protein, a great source of fibre, and packing a flavour-punch. This is the way every day should start.

SUPER TOFU & VEG SCRAMBLE ON TOAST

SERVES 2

300g smoked (or plain) tofu
2 tablespoons sunflower oil
1 medium red onion, peeled and
  finely chopped
2 teaspoons smoked paprika
1 teaspoon ground cumin
½ teaspoon ground turmeric
75g mushrooms, cleaned and
  sliced
8 cherry tomatoes, halved
3 garlic cloves, peeled and
  minced or grated
½ teaspoon wholegrain mustard
1–2 green chillies, deseeded and
  finely sliced (optional)
1 teaspoon salt

TO SERVE

4 slices of wholemeal bread
vegan butter
3 spring onions, thinly sliced

1. Remove the excess liquid from the tofu by wrapping it in a clean tea towel and either pressing it under a heavy book or wringing it out.
2. Heat the oil in a large non-stick frying pan over a medium heat. Add the onion and cook gently until soft. Stir in the smoked paprika, cumin and turmeric, and cook for a further minute.
3. Stir in the mushrooms, tomatoes, garlic, mustard, chillies and salt, and cook for another 3–4 minutes until the mushrooms have softened.
4. Finally, crumble the tofu and add it to the pan, stirring to coat it in the other ingredients. Let it cook for another 4–5 minutes until it has warmed through.
5. Meanwhile, toast the bread and spread it with vegan butter.
6. Serve the tofu on the toast and garnish with the spring onions.

Tip: If you miss the eggy flavour, add ¼ teaspoon of crushed kala namak, also known as black salt, when you add the spices.

A note on chillies: The standard chillies available in supermarkets often have little heat. If you prefer more, try finger or bird's-eye chillies, and if you want still more, leave the seeds in! If you like less heat, use fewer or milder chillies.

If cereal and toast fail to float your boat, try this delight for breakfast. It takes just ten minutes to cook and sets you up for the day with the power of fresh avocados, the sweetness of corn, and a zingy hit of chilli and lime. Delicious.

BAKED AVOCADOS WITH HOT & SPICY CORN SALSA

SERVES 2

100g sweetcorn kernels (tinned or frozen and defrosted)
2 spring onions, finely sliced
50g cherry tomatoes, quartered
1 tablespoon fresh coriander, chopped
½ lime, zest and juice
1–2 tablespoons hot pepper sauce
2 just-ripe avocados, halved and with the stones removed

1. Heat the oven to 180°C fan/400°F/Gas Mark 6.
2. In a bowl, mix together all the ingredients except the avocados.
3. Place the avocados on a baking tray cut side up and load each half with the salsa mix. Bake for 10 minutes.
4. Remove from the oven and serve.

This is a recipe that loves to be adapted. If you like chives, marjoram, tarragon or thyme, use those instead of the dill and parsley we have suggested. Switch wholegrain mustard for Dijon, or leave it out altogether. Double up on the smoked paprika if that's a flavour you particularly love, or sprinkle some chilli flakes or nutritional yeast flakes on at the end. Whatever you do, these mushrooms will soak the flavours right up, and you'll have wonderfully deliciously creamy mushrooms to start your day.

CREAMY HERBED MUSHROOMS ON TOAST

SERVES 2

1 onion, peeled and finely diced
1 tablespoon olive oil
400g chestnut mushrooms, cleaned and sliced
2 garlic cloves, peeled and minced or grated
½ teaspoon salt
1 teaspoon paprika
½ teaspoon smoked paprika
100ml soya or oat cream
1 teaspoon wholegrain mustard
10g fresh parsley, finely chopped
5g fresh dill, finely chopped
salt and pepper, to taste

TO SERVE
4 slices of sourdough or your favourite bread
vegan butter (optional)

1. Fry the onion in the oil over a medium heat for 8–10 minutes, until beginning to soften.
2. Add the mushrooms, garlic, salt, paprika and smoked paprika, and fry for another 5 minutes, stirring.
3. When the mushrooms are soft, remove from the heat and stir in the soya or oat cream, the mustard and most of the chopped herbs. (Note, tarragon is a very strong flavour, so if you are using this you may wish to reduce the amount.) Season to taste.
4. Toast the bread, spread with the vegan butter if you are using it, and heap on the mushrooms. Sprinkle the rest of the herbs over the top and serve.

Traditionally a fusion of Asian spices and smoked fish, we've updated one or two things for our vegan version, freshening it up with lemon zest and creamy coconut yoghurt. We think you'll love this any time of day.

KEDGEREE WITH HERBY YOGHURT

SERVES 4

2 tablespoons sunflower oil
1 onion, peeled and finely
    chopped
1–3 green chillies, deseeded and
    finely chopped
1 tablespoon curry powder
½ teaspoon ground turmeric
2.5cm piece of fresh ginger,
    peeled and grated
300g basmati rice
600ml vegetable stock
1 bay leaf
225g smoked tofu, drained and
    crumbled
a handful of fresh parsley,
    chopped
1 lemon, zest only

TO SERVE
toasted flaked almonds
a handful of fresh coriander,
    finely chopped
150g coconut yoghurt

1. Heat the oil in a large pan and gently fry the onions for 7–8 minutes, until soft.
2. Add the chillies, curry powder, turmeric and ginger, and mix well. Let it cook for another 2–3 minutes, stirring every now and then.
3. Stir in the rice, and coat it with the spices. Add the stock and the bay leaf and bring to the boil. Cover with a lid, reduce the heat and let it simmer for 10 minutes.
4. Remove from the heat and leave to stand for another 10 minutes. Don't lift the lid!
5. Add the crumbled tofu to the rice along with the parsley and lemon zest. Garnish with flaked almonds.
6. In a bowl, stir the coriander into the yoghurt, and serve alongside the kedgeree.

A note on chillies: The standard chillies available in supermarkets often have little heat. If you prefer more, try finger or bird's-eye chillies, and if you want still more, leave the seeds in! If you like less heat, use fewer or milder chillies.

This is a lovely, layered breakfast, made with frozen banana, fresh fruits and a peanut butter granola. The granola will keep for 2–3 weeks in an airtight container, and you can refreeze the banana ice cream, so make the components ahead of time to keep your mornings stress-free. It's also fine to use shop-bought granola, of course, or you might like to add a layer of coconut yoghurt. So many options!

PEANUT BUTTER BREAKFAST SUNDAES

SERVES 4

FOR THE GRANOLA
65g oats
55g mixed nut pieces
½ teaspoon ground cinnamon
¼ teaspoon salt
85g peanut butter
1 tablespoon black treacle
1 tablespoon agave syrup
1½ tablespoons coconut oil (or vegetable oil)
1 teaspoon vanilla extract

FOR THE BANANA ICE CREAM
2 bananas, peeled, chopped and frozen overnight
50g blueberries, plus another 100g to top the sundaes, washed
¼ teaspoon vanilla extract
a little almond or coconut milk

TO SERVE (OPTIONAL)
toasted chopped hazelnuts
a drizzle of agave syrup

1. Make the granola first. Heat the oven to 160°C fan/350°F/Gas Mark 4.
2. In a bowl, mix together the oats, nuts, cinnamon and salt.
3. In a saucepan, combine the peanut butter, black treacle, agave syrup, coconut oil and vanilla extract. Warm it on the hob to ensure the ingredients soften and mix fully together.
4. Pour the peanut butter mixture into the oat mixture and stir until fully combined.
5. Line a baking tray with baking parchment and spread the mixture out on it. Bake for 18–20 minutes, stirring halfway through.
6. Remove from the oven and set aside to allow it to crisp up as it cools completely.
7. Now, blitz the frozen bananas with 50g of the blueberries and the vanilla extract until smooth, adding just enough milk to help it break down and form a smooth soft-serve mixture.
8. Assemble your sundae by layering the granola and banana ice cream. Top with the remaining blueberries and the hazelnuts, plus a drizzle of agave syrup if you would like a little more sweetness.

We'll be honest. We called this a breakfast burrito because it's a hearty, portable meal that sets up the day perfectly, but it works as a brunch, lunch, light meal or snack, too. The cumin-spiced chickpeas alongside the fresh leaves and that hit of hot pepper make this a favourite whatever time of day (or night) you eat it. The filling can be made ahead of time and kept in the refrigerator ready to assemble whenever you want it.

BREAKFAST BURRITO WITH SRIRACHA MAYO

MAKES 2

FOR THE CUMIN-SPICED CHICKPEAS
1 small red onion, peeled and finely diced
a little olive oil
2 garlic cloves, peeled and minced or grated
1 teaspoon ground cumin
1 teaspoon paprika
½ teaspoon dried oregano
½ teaspoon salt
1 x 400g tin of chickpeas, drained and rinsed

FOR THE SRIRACHA MAYO
35g vegan mayonnaise
1 tablespoon sriracha sauce (less if you prefer less of a kick)
a squeeze of lime juice
a dash of soy sauce

TO SERVE
2 large wholewheat wraps
1 ripe avocado, peeled, stone removed and sliced
a handful of rocket

1. To make the spiced chickpeas, fry the onion in the olive oil until soft. Add the garlic and cook for another minute, stirring.
2. Add the cumin, paprika, oregano and salt, and mix well. Stir in the chickpeas and cook for another 2–3 minutes, roughly mashing the chickpeas with the back of the spoon. Remove from the heat.
3. Combine the ingredients for the sriracha mayo in a bowl, then stir into the chickpeas.
4. Warm the wraps in the microwave for 30 seconds, or in a dry frying pan.
5. Assemble your burrito! Load the mayo-covered spiced chickpeas, avocado and rocket on to the wrap, and fold it up like a burrito pro.

2.

MAINS

OK, so we've taken a few liberties with the traditional dish. We have coconut bacon instead of meat, cashews in place of the eggs, and vegan parmesan to replace the dairy version. We have also freshened it up with a pop of bright green peas. Multitaskers will be able to make the three elements – the bacon, sauce and pasta – all at once, but you could also do them one at a time, leaving the pasta until last.

CREAMY CARBONARA WITH COCONUT BACON

SERVES 4

FOR THE COCONUT BACON
50g coconut flakes of roughly
    uniform size
½ tablespoon sunflower oil
1 tablespoon soy sauce
½ teaspoon smoked paprika
½ teaspoon liquid smoke
salt and pepper, to taste

FOR THE CARBONARA
3 shallots, peeled and finely
    chopped
2 tablespoons olive oil
3 garlic cloves, peeled and
    finely sliced
150g frozen peas
125g cashew nuts
150ml unsweetened plant milk
3 tablespoons nutritional yeast
salt and pepper, to taste

FOR THE PASTA
350g spaghetti
vegan parmesan, to serve
    (optional)

1. Heat the oven to 160°C fan/350°F/Gas Mark 4.
2. Mix all the bacon ingredients together in a bowl, ensuring the coconut flakes are well coated. Spread them out on a baking tray lined with baking parchment and bake for 12 minutes, keeping an eye on them and stirring halfway through to prevent them burning. Remove from the oven and set aside.
3. While the bacon is in the oven, bring a pan of water to the boil and cook the spaghetti as per the packet instructions.
4. While the pasta is cooking, make the carbonara. In a large pan, over a medium heat, fry the shallots in the olive oil for about 5 minutes, until softening. Add the garlic and fry for 2 minutes, then add the peas and cook for another minute or two, stirring every now and then. Remove from the heat and set aside.
5. Blend the cashews with the plant milk until you get a creamy smooth mixture. Stir in the nutritional yeast, mixing well, then combine with the shallots and peas. You can add a little water if you prefer a looser consistency. Season to taste.
6. When the spaghetti is cooked, drain it and coat it in the creamy mixture. Scatter as much of the coconut bacon as you'd like on top, and add a sprinkling of grated vegan parmesan, if using.

Two tips to simplify further: If making coconut bacon is a step too far, use shop-bought vegan bacon or sprinkle some 'bacon bits' on instead – most of those you find in supermarkets are vegan. And if you don't have a high-speed blender to blitz the cashews, you can save yourself some time by using 175ml of vegan cream in place of the cashews and plant milk.

We wanted to bring you a delicious burger but couldn't decide whether to base it on peanuts or beans, so we invented the BeaNut Burger™. We used crunchy peanut butter and black beans, but you can use any nut butter and any type of bean, and you can tweak the spices to your own preference. This is a great way to get more plants into your diet while still enjoying super tasty indulgent food. (We didn't actually trademark the name, but we were quite proud of ourselves for coming up with that pun. Please forgive us.)

BEANUT BURGER

SERVES 4

3 tablespoons sunflower oil
1 onion, peeled and finely diced
1 garlic clove, peeled and
    minced or grated
½ teaspoon ground cumin
½ teaspoon cayenne
2 tablespoons crunchy
    peanut butter
1 medium carrot, peeled
    and grated
1 x 400g tin of black beans,
    drained, rinsed and roughly
    mashed with a fork
salt and pepper, to taste

1. Heat half the oil in a pan, then add the onions and gently fry them over a medium heat until they are softening – around 7–8 minutes.
2. Add the garlic, cumin and cayenne, and cook for another 2–3 minutes.
3. Stir in the peanut butter and let it warm until it softens.
4. Stir in the grated carrot and mashed black beans and mix well to combine.
5. Remove from the heat and season to taste. When cool enough to handle, shape into four patties, pressing them together. (You can use some flour on your hands if the mixture is a little sticky.)
6. Fry the burgers in the remaining oil for around 5 minutes, then turn them over carefully and cook for another 2–3 minutes.
7. Serve your BeaNut Burger™ in a bun with your choice of pickles, vegan mayo, mustard, ketchup, vegan cheese, lettuce and tomato.

This is like a shepherd's pie but (in our view) tastier and with a much cooler name. The aduki beans provide the fibre-rich protein, and the creamy mashed potatoes bring the 'aahhh' factor. Serve with green vegetables for a classic family favourite.

RED DRAGON PIE

SERVES 4–6

1.25kg potatoes, peeled and roughly chopped
2 tablespoons vegan butter
1 medium leek, cleaned and sliced
2 tablespoons olive oil
2 garlic cloves, peeled and minced or grated
150g mushrooms, sliced
1 red pepper, deseeded and chopped
2 large carrots, peeled and finely diced
3 x 400g tins of aduki beans, drained and rinsed
1 teaspoon dried thyme
a handful of fresh parsley, chopped
salt and pepper, to taste
a glug of red wine (around 100ml, optional)
375ml vegetable stock
2 tablespoons tomato purée
1 heaped tablespoon cornflour
50g vegan cheese, grated (choose a type that melts)

1. Heat the oven to 180°C fan/400°F/Gas Mark 6.
2. Bring a large pan of water to the boil and cook the potatoes until soft. Drain, then mash with the vegan butter and season with black pepper. Set aside.
3. Meanwhile, in a large pan, fry the leek gently in the olive oil until soft. Add the garlic and mushrooms and cook for a further 2 minutes, stirring to ensure the garlic does not burn.
4. Add the red pepper, carrots, beans and herbs. Stir well, then season to taste.
5. Add the glug of wine (if using) and the stock. Cover and turn the heat up to bring it to the boil, then take the lid off and let it simmer for 6-8 minutes, or until the carrots are soft. Stir in the tomato purée.
6. In a small dish, mix the cornflour with 2 tablespoons of cold water, then stir it into the boiling liquid to thicken it into a tasty gravy.
7. Remove the pan from the heat and pour the bean mixture into a baking dish. Cover with the mashed potato and sprinkle over the vegan cheese. Place in the oven for 25-30 minutes, until the top is starting to brown.
8. Remove from the oven and serve.

Note: Not every vegan cheese melts in the oven, though they seem happy to do so under the grill. If you want that melted cheese top, put the cheese on AFTER the pie has come out of the oven and pop it under a hot grill for 2–3 minutes.

Don't be put off by the number of ingredients here, because making the curry paste from scratch is a total game-changer. And after all, those ingredients just go into a blender and get blitzed, so it's not as complex as it might look. But if time is tight, go right ahead and use a shop-bought Thai green paste instead, making sure you have one that does not contain fish. Serve with rice or noodles, or just as it is in a beautiful big steaming bowl.

THAI GREEN CURRY

SERVES 4

FOR THE THAI GREEN PASTE
6 shallots, peeled and roughly
    chopped
4 garlic cloves, peeled
2–4 green finger chillies, roughly
    chopped (depending on how
    much heat you like)
6cm piece of fresh ginger, peeled
    and grated
2 sticks of lemongrass, tough
    outer leaves removed, finely
    chopped
1 teaspoon ground cumin
2 tablespoons dark soy sauce
a handful of fresh coriander

FOR THE CURRY
125g green beans
125g asparagus
2 tablespoons sunflower oil
400g firm plain tofu, drained and
    cut into 1cm cubes
125g baby corn, sliced in half
    lengthways
125g pak choi, leaves separated
1 x 400ml tin of coconut milk
2 tablespoons soy sauce
1 tablespoon cornflour, mixed
    with just enough water to
    form a smooth paste

TO SERVE
1 lime, juice only
2 spring onions, cut into
    thin slices
fresh coriander

1. Put the shallots, garlic, chillies and ginger into a food processor and blitz. Add the lemongrass, cumin, soy sauce and coriander, and blitz again, pausing to scrape the mixture from the sides if necessary.
2. Blanch the green beans and asparagus in boiling water for 1 minute, then drain and refresh under cold water.
3. Heat the oil in a wok and add the green paste. Cook for 4–5 minutes, stirring occasionally. This will smell AMAZING.
4. Add the tofu and stir to coat with the paste. Cook for another 5 minutes, stirring occasionally.
5. Add the beans, asparagus, baby corn and pak choi, then the coconut milk and soy sauce. Cover and bring to the boil, then turn the heat down and let it simmer for another 4–5 minutes.
6. Stir in the cornflour paste and let it boil for another minute to thicken the sauce, then remove from the heat.
7. Squeeze in the lime juice and serve sprinkled with the spring onions and fresh coriander.

A note on chillies: The standard chillies available in supermarkets often have little heat. If you prefer more, try finger or bird's-eye chillies, and if you want still more, leave the seeds in! If you like less heat, use fewer or milder chillies.

It's no exaggeration to say that discovering gochujang, that well-loved Korean chilli sauce, has changed our lives. This is our own take on it, and when cooked with roasted cauliflower, and cooled by the mint mayo drizzle, it creates one of the very tastiest – and simplest – meals. Would we eat this every day? Probably. *See photo overleaf.*

GOCHUJANG ROASTED CAULIFLOWER WITH HERBED QUINOA & MINT MAYO DRIZZLE

SERVES 4

FOR THE GOCHUJANG SAUCE
2 teaspoons dried chilli flakes
    (halve this for less of a kick)
1 teaspoon paprika
1 teaspoon smoked paprika
2 tablespoons brown or red
    miso paste
2 tablespoons agave syrup
2 tablespoons tamari or dark
    soy sauce
2 tablespoons toasted sesame oil
1 small garlic clove, peeled and
    finely grated

FOR THE CAULIFLOWER
1 large cauliflower, trimmed,
    leaving the core intact, and
    cut into 3cm thick slices

FOR THE HERBED QUINOA
200g quinoa
1 vegetable stock cube or
    1 teaspoon bouillon powder
2 shallots, peeled and finely
    chopped
50g pine nuts
1 tablespoon each of fresh
    parsley, mint and dill, chopped
1 lemon, zest plus half the juice

FOR THE MINT MAYO DRIZZLE
50g vegan mayonnaise
¼ cucumber, grated
4–5 fresh mint leaves, finely chopped
salt and pepper, to taste

1. Heat the oven to 220°C fan/475°F/Gas Mark 9.
2. Make the gochujang sauce by mixing together all the ingredients in a bowl. Set aside.
3. Lay the cauliflower slices on a baking tray. Spread half the gochujang sauce over one side, then turn them over and spread the rest on the other side. Cover the dish with tin foil and bake for 5 minutes. Remove the foil and bake for another 15–18 minutes, turning the cauliflower halfway through.
4. Meanwhile, cook the quinoa as per the packet instructions, adding the stock cube or bouillon powder to the water. When cooked, add the remaining quinoa ingredients and set aside.
5. Finally, make the mint mayo drizzle by mixing together the ingredients in a bowl.
6. When ready, serve the slices of cauliflower on top of the quinoa, with the mint mayo drizzled over the top.

In this winning dish, the roasted potatoes and tofu are the building blocks, the green beans bring the crunch, and then comes the deliciously warming peanut sauce and a spicy sambal chutney on the side. What's not to love?

SATAY TRAYBAKE WITH SMOKED TOFU & SPICY SAMBAL

SERVES 2

FOR THE TRAYBAKE

225–250g smoked tofu, cut into
    2cm cubes
350g small new potatoes, scrubbed
    and halved lengthways
2 tablespoons olive oil
salt and pepper, to taste
150g green beans, topped and tailed
200g beansprouts, rinsed

FOR THE SAMBAL

5 round shallots, peeled and
    roughly chopped
1 garlic clove, peeled
1 teaspoon lemongrass purée
2 red chillies (deseeded if you
    prefer less heat)
1 tablespoon sunflower oil,
    plus a little more if needed
a pinch of ground turmeric
1 teaspoon sugar
a pinch of salt
a squeeze of lime juice

FOR THE SATAY SAUCE

65g peanut butter
1 garlic clove, peeled and
    minced or grated
1 red chilli, finely chopped
    (deseeded if you prefer
    less heat)
175ml coconut milk
1 teaspoon brown sugar
1 tablespoon soy sauce
1 teaspoon grated fresh ginger
a squeeze of lime juice

1. Start by making the sambal. In a food processor, blitz the shallots, garlic, lemongrass purée and chillies, adding a little oil to the mix if it won't break down easily. It should still have plenty of texture.

2. Warm the sunflower oil in a frying pan over a medium heat, then add the blended shallot mixture. Add the turmeric, and let it cook gently for 15 minutes, stirring occasionally to ensure it does not stick.

3. Finally, add the sugar and salt, and cook for a further 5 minutes. Remove the sambal from the heat and stir in the lime juice. Set aside.

4. Meanwhile, heat the oven to 200°C fan/425°F/Gas Mark 7.

5. Put the tofu and potatoes into a large roasting tray and turn them over in the olive oil. Season to taste, then put them into the oven for 20–25 minutes.

6. Add the green beans and beansprouts to the roasting tray and stir well, adding a drizzle more oil if you are worried the potatoes will stick. Put the tray back into the oven for another 12–15 minutes.

7. While the vegetables and tofu finish roasting, make the satay sauce by putting all the ingredients except the lime juice into a small saucepan, and warming it over a gentle heat, stirring until it becomes smooth.

8. Remove from the heat and add the lime juice.

9. Serve the roasted tofu and vegetables with the peanut sauce drizzled over the top, and with the spicy sambal on the side.

A note on chillies: The standard chillies available in supermarkets often have little heat. If you prefer more, try finger or bird's-eye chillies, and if you want still more, leave the seeds in! If you like less heat, use fewer or milder chillies.

Admittedly this recipe takes a little time, but if you're a multi-tasker it's possible to create all three elements alongside each other, which makes a prep time of about 45 minutes, followed by 40 minutes for the lasagne to cook. So it may not be a midweek dinner, but it does make a lovely weekend meal for family, housemates or visiting friends. Serve it with a dressed green salad in summer or with a hunk of garlic bread in winter. Purists won't add cheese to the béchamel, but if you like it, go ahead and add it.

ROASTED AUBERGINE & RED PEPPER LASAGNE

SERVES 4

FOR THE AUBERGINES
2 aubergines, sliced lengthways into 1cm thick slices
1 red pepper, deseeded and diced
3 large garlic cloves, unpeeled and left whole
olive oil
salt and pepper, to taste
1 pack of dried lasagne sheets

FOR THE TOMATO SAUCE
1 red onion, peeled and sliced
250g brown or Puy lentils
2 x 400g tins of chopped tomatoes
2 tablespoons sun-dried tomato paste or tomato purée
150ml vegetable stock
a glug of red wine (optional)
1 teaspoon dried thyme leaves (or 2 teaspoons fresh)
black pepper, to taste

FOR THE BÉCHAMEL
50g vegan butter
50g plain flour
550ml plant milk
1 bay leaf

1. Heat the oven to 200°C fan/425°F/Gas Mark 7.
2. Place the aubergines, red peppers and whole garlic cloves in a single layer on a roasting tray (or two trays if they don't fit), drizzle them with olive oil, and season with salt and pepper. Roast for 20 minutes, then turn the vegetables over and roast for another 20 minutes. Remove from the oven.
3. Meanwhile, make the tomato sauce. In a large pan, fry the onion in a little more olive oil until it starts to soften – about 7–8 minutes. Add the lentils, tinned tomatoes, tomato paste or purée, stock, red wine (if using) and thyme. Let it simmer for about 20 minutes, stirring every now and then to prevent sticking. When the liquid has reduced significantly, remove the pan from the heat, season with black pepper, and set aside.
4. When the vegetables have roasted, pop the garlic cloves out of their skins, taking care as they will still be hot, and stir them into the tomato sauce, breaking them up if possible. Stir in the roasted vegetables, not worrying if the aubergines break up, and set the pan aside.
5. Now, make the béchamel. Melt the vegan butter in a saucepan and add the flour until it becomes a paste, stirring continuously. Let it cook gently for a minute or two, then remove from the heat.
6. Add the plant milk a little at a time, stirring until it is all fully mixed, without lumps. Add the bay leaf and put the pan back on the heat, stirring continuously. The sauce will thicken as it warms and by the time it reaches a simmer, it should be ready. Remove from the heat, remove the bay leaf, and season to taste.
7. Now, you're ready to assemble. Spoon a third of the tomato sauce into the bottom of a deep ovenproof dish. Cover with lasagne sheets, breaking pieces to fill in any gaps, then spoon a third of the béchamel on top. Repeat to create two more layers, finishing with a layer of béchamel.
8. Bake for 35–40 minutes, or until golden and bubbling. Remove from the oven and let it stand for 5 minutes before serving.

We love mac & cheese in any form, and this version – which is just a little bit fancy – is a firm family favourite. With that comforting cheesy sauce and the lovely Mediterranean flavours, it's bound to please your family, too. Serve it with a green salad or your choice of fresh veggies.

SMOKY MEDITERRANEAN MAC & CHEESE

SERVES 4

125g cashew nuts
300g macaroni or your pasta of
    choice
1 medium onion, peeled and
    finely diced
2 tablespoons olive oil
3 garlic cloves, peeled and
    minced or grated
6 sun-dried tomatoes
175g roasted red peppers (from
    a jar)
½ tablespoon tomato purée
1 teaspoon Dijon mustard
1 tablespoon white miso paste
1 teaspoon smoked paprika
1 teaspoon liquid smoke
    (optional)
2 tablespoons nutritional yeast
400ml vegetable stock
75g vegan cheese, grated
    (optional, but choose one
    that melts)

1. If you don't have a high-speed blender, soak the cashews for 2 hours, then drain.
2. Heat the oven to 200°C fan/425°F/Gas Mark 7.
3. Cook the macaroni as per the packet instructions, then drain and set aside.
4. Meanwhile, fry the onion in the olive oil until soft – about 7–8 minutes – then add the garlic and cook for another 2 minutes.
5. Put the onions and garlic into a blender with the sun-dried tomatoes, red peppers, tomato purée, mustard, miso, smoked paprika, liquid smoke (if using), nutritional yeast and stock. Add the drained cashews and blend until smooth. (This could take a few minutes, especially if your blender is not a high-speed one.)
6. Put the sauce back into the pan you have already used, and warm it over a medium heat for a few minutes to let it thicken a bit. Stir in the macaroni.
7. Now, heap the macaroni and sauce into either one large dish or four individual ones, sprinkle on the cheese (if using) and cook in the oven for 15–20 minutes. The cheese should have melted, and the top will be just starting to brown.
8. Remove from the oven and serve.

The sweet and smoky potatoes alongside the deliciously rich mole (a traditional Mexican sauce of black beans and spices) are a match made in vegan heaven. It's a nourishing and filling meal, and it's super tasty too.

BLACK BEAN MOLE WITH SWEET POTATO FRIES

SERVES 4

FOR THE MOLE
2 tablespoons vegetable oil
1 medium onion, peeled and finely diced
1 large carrot, peeled and finely diced
2 garlic cloves, peeled and minced or grated
2 teaspoons ground cumin
2 teaspoons ground coriander
2 teaspoons paprika
1 teaspoon ground cinnamon
1 teaspoon dried chipotle chilli flakes
1 teaspoon dried oregano
2 x 400g tins of black beans
1 x 400g tin of tomatoes
1 bay leaf
1 tablespoon cocoa powder
100ml vegetable stock

FOR THE FRIES
750g sweet potatoes, peeled and cut into 1cm thick wedges
3 tablespoons olive oil
1 tablespoon smoked paprika
2 teaspoons salt

1. Start with the mole. Heat the oil in a large pan, add the onion and carrot, and fry over a medium heat for 5 minutes.
2. Add the garlic, spices and oregano, and stir for another minute.
3. Add the black beans, tomatoes, bay leaf, cocoa powder and stock. Cover and bring to the boil, then turn down the heat and let it simmer for 5 minutes. Set aside.
4. Heat the oven to 220°C fan/475°F/Gas Mark 9 and put a large baking tray inside to heat.
5. Toss the sweet potato wedges in the oil and coat with the paprika and salt.
6. Spread them on the heated baking tray and bake for 20–25 minutes, removing from the oven and turning the fries with tongs halfway through.
7. Serve the sweet potatoes with the mole, remembering to remove the bay leaf!

Bao buns are easier to make than you might think. You'll need some baking parchment and a bamboo steamer, and the dough will need 1–2 hours to rise, but if you plan ahead, you will be truly rewarded. These super tasty, mushroom-filled steamed buns are perfect with the colourful, crunchy slaw. Give them a try!

HOISIN MUSHROOM BAO BUNS WITH AN ASIAN-STYLE SLAW

SERVES 4

FOR THE BAO BUNS
225ml warm water
1¼ teaspoons dried active yeast
350g plain flour
1½ tablespoons sugar
1 teaspoon salt
1 teaspoon baking powder
1 tablespoon sunflower oil, plus a
    little more

FOR THE MUSHROOM FILLING
1 small red onion, peeled and
    finely diced
2 tablespoons sunflower oil
350g mushrooms, halved and
    sliced
2 garlic cloves, peeled and
    minced or grated
3 tablespoons soy sauce
2 tablespoons rice wine vinegar
3 tablespoons sriracha sauce
1 tablespoon maple or agave
    syrup
1 tablespoon hoisin sauce

FOR THE SLAW
200g red cabbage, finely sliced
1 little gem lettuce, shredded
2 carrots, peeled and grated
4 spring onions, sliced diagonally
a handful of fresh Thai basil, torn
    (if available)
3 tablespoons sesame oil
2 tablespoons soy sauce
2 tablespoons agave or maple
    syrup
1 teaspoon grated fresh ginger
fresh coriander, to serve
    (optional)

1. Start by making the dough for the buns. Whisk together the water and yeast in a small bowl, then set aside.

2. In a larger bowl, mix the flour, sugar, salt and baking powder, then stir in 1 tablespoon of the oil.

3. Add the wet mixture to the dry ingredients, then combine to form a soft dough. Transfer to a lightly floured work surface and knead until it is smooth and elastic (about 7–8 minutes).

4. Grease a bowl using a little more oil. Roll the dough into a ball, put it into the bowl, and cover it with a clean tea towel. Leave it in a warm spot to rise until it has doubled in size (about 1–2 hours).

5. Meanwhile, make the mushroom filling. Fry the onion in the oil over a medium heat until soft, then add the mushrooms and garlic. Cook for 2–3 minutes, stirring.

6. Add the rest of the filling ingredients, then turn up the heat to medium-high and cook for a further 5–6 minutes until everything is soft. (The mushrooms will yield fluid, so don't worry if it seems a bit dry to start with.) Set aside to let it cool.

7. Make the slaw by combining the vegetables in a large bowl and the rest of the ingredients (apart from the coriander) in a small one to make the dressing. Pour the dressing over the vegetables and refrigerate until you are ready to use it.

8. With the dough doubled in size, divide it into ten equal pieces. Roll the first one into a ball, flatten it with your hand, then roll it out to a 10–12cm round. Holding it flat in the palm of your hand, put 1 tablespoon of the cooled mushroom mixture into the middle, then fold the outsides in, pinching and twisting until it forms a little sealed parcel that looks like an old-fashioned drawstring money bag. Repeat with the rest of the filling and dough.

9. Put some baking parchment into a bamboo steamer – enough for the buns to sit on but not so much that it covers the entire bottom of the steamer, as we need space for the steam to circulate. Place the buns in the steamer and steam them for 8 minutes over a pan of boiling water. (Unless you have a huge bamboo steamer, you will need to do this in batches.)

10. When cooked, serve the buns with the slaw, and a sprinkle of fresh coriander (if using).

This family favourite takes moments to prepare, uses just one pot, and you barely need to tend to it while it's in the oven. It couldn't be easier, but don't let its simplicity fool you. It's also really tasty. Serve just as it is, or with some steamed broccoli and gravy.

SAUSAGE & NEW POTATO TRAYBAKE

SERVES 2

6 frozen vegan sausages
350g new potatoes, scrubbed and cut into small bite-size chunks
2 leeks, cleaned and sliced
1 teaspoon fresh rosemary, finely chopped
4 tablespoons olive oil
2 teaspoons wholegrain mustard
1 teaspoon agave syrup
salt and pepper, to taste

1. Heat the oven to 200°C fan/425°F/Gas Mark 7.
2. Put the sausages, potatoes, leeks and rosemary into a roasting dish.
3. In a bowl, mix together the oil, mustard and agave syrup, then pour into the roasting dish and mix well.
4. Season with salt and pepper and bake for 35–45 minutes, or until the potatoes are cooked, stirring after 20 minutes. The exact cooking time will depend on the size of your 'bite-size' potatoes.
5. Remove from the oven and serve.

There are hundreds of options for the centrepiece of a roast dinner – from slices of faux roast meat (available in stores) to a lentil loaf, and from a rosemary-seasoned Brazil nut roast to a chestnut and red wine puff pie. But this wellington is up there with the best of them. It looks impressive and tastes just as good. Serve with roast potatoes, fresh vegetables, stuffing and gravy for the full experience. *See photo overleaf.*

MUSHROOM & WALNUT WELLINGTON (FOR THE PERFECT ROAST DINNER)

SERVES 6

2 tablespoons sunflower oil
½ medium onion, peeled and finely diced
2 sticks of celery, finely chopped
2 small carrots, peeled and finely diced
3 garlic cloves, peeled and minced or grated
1 teaspoon dried thyme
1 teaspoon dried rosemary
250g mushrooms, finely diced
2 tablespoons soy sauce
2 tablespoons tomato purée
1 x 400g tin of chickpeas, drained, rinsed and mashed with a fork
100g walnuts, broken into very small pieces
100g ground almonds
salt and pepper, to taste
1 sheet of ready-rolled puff pastry (around 350g)
a little melted vegan butter or some plant milk to glaze

1. Heat the oven to 200°C fan/425°F/Gas Mark 7.
2. In a large pan, heat the oil and fry the onion, celery and carrots for 8–10 minutes, stirring intermittently.
3. Add the garlic and herbs and cook for another minute, then add the mushrooms and cook until they are soft – another 5–6 minutes. Remove from the heat.
4. Stir in the soy sauce, tomato purée, mashed chickpeas, walnut pieces and ground almonds, and combine well. It should form a moist but thick mixture that can be shaped with your hands. (If it is too wet, add additional ground almonds, or some oats or breadcrumbs.) Season with salt and pepper.
5. Cover a baking sheet with baking parchment and lay the pastry sheet on top. Using your hands, shape the mushroom mixture into a long sausage shape along the middle of the pastry, leaving a small gap at each end.
6. Wrap one side of the pastry over the loaf, then the other. Gently press to seal it, using a little plant milk to help it stick. Now roll in the ends and fold it like a burrito. Turn the wellington over so the folds are facing downwards.
7. Brush the top with melted vegan butter or a little more plant milk, then gently cut diagonal slits in the pastry about 2cm apart.
8. Cook for 35 minutes, until the pastry is golden brown. Remove from the oven and serve.

Mushrooms are amazing. Not only do they soak up flavours and give this recipe that delicious umami taste, but they're also a fantastic source of vitamin D, which makes them an important mood booster too. Here we use both chestnut mushrooms and fancy porcini for double the health benefit and double the flavour.

MUSHROOM BOLOGNESE

SERVES 4

10g dried porcini mushrooms (optional)
1 onion, peeled and diced
2 tablespoons olive oil
2 garlic cloves, peeled and minced or grated
250g chestnut mushrooms, finely diced
1 red pepper, deseeded and diced
1 stick of celery, thinly sliced
300g frozen soya mince
1 teaspoon dried oregano
1 x 400g tin of tomatoes
125ml red wine
2 tablespoons sun-dried tomato paste (or chopped sun-dried tomatoes)
1 tablespoon tomato purée
2 tablespoons dark soy sauce
200ml vegetable stock (incorporating the soaking water from the porcini, if using)
1 bay leaf
salt and pepper, to taste
350g spaghetti or pappardelle
2 tablespoons olive oil
a handful of fresh basil (optional)

1. Rehydrate the dried porcini as per the packet instructions, then cut them up into tiny pieces, reserving the liquid.
2. Fry the onion in the olive oil until it softens – about 6–7 minutes. Then add the garlic, chestnut mushrooms, porcini mushrooms, red pepper and celery, and cook for another 3–4 minutes.
3. Add the soya mince and oregano and stir well.
4. Finally, add the tinned tomatoes, red wine, sun-dried tomato paste, tomato purée, soy sauce, vegetable stock (plus the porcini water) and bay leaf. Stir well, and season to taste.
5. Cover with a lid and bring to the boil, then reduce the heat and simmer for 15 minutes, until the sauce has reduced and thickened.
6. Meanwhile, cook the pasta as per the packet instructions. Drain it, stir in a glug of olive oil, and serve with the mushroom sauce. Add some fresh torn basil leaves if you like.

Tip: If your sauce hasn't thickened as much as you would like, stir in ½–1 tablespoon of vegan gravy granules right at the end of the cooking time but while it is still boiling.

For this beautiful curry we have used sweet potatoes, butternut squash and green beans, but you can use any vegetables you like or replace one of them with cubes of tofu. Making the paste from scratch may seem like a bit of an effort, but really you just throw everything into the blender, and it's done. And for this, you are rewarded with a fragrant, spicy, coconutty curry that really is hard to beat.

CAMBODIAN SAMLÁ-STYLE CURRY

SERVES 4

FOR THE CURRY PASTE
2 sticks of lemongrass, peeled and finely chopped
2 shallots, peeled and roughly chopped
4 garlic cloves, peeled
5cm piece of fresh ginger, peeled and roughly chopped
2–4 chillies (leave the seeds in if you want more heat)
2 limes, zest only
6 fresh mint leaves
1 teaspoon ground turmeric
1 teaspoon salt

FOR THE CURRY
2 tablespoons sunflower oil
500ml vegetable stock
3 tablespoons light soy sauce
1 tablespoon brown sugar
500g sweet potatoes, peeled and cut into bite-size pieces
300g butternut squash, peeled and cut into bite-size pieces
125g green beans, topped and tailed
50g creamed coconut
50g roasted salted peanuts, roughly chopped
2 tablespoons fresh mint leaves, chopped

1. Place all the ingredients for the curry paste in a blender and blitz until smooth. (If the mixture is too dry to blitz, add a little water.)
2. Heat the sunflower oil in a large pan, and fry the paste for 3–4 minutes. Add the stock, soy sauce and brown sugar. Bring to the boil, add the sweet potatoes and butternut squash, then cover and let it simmer for 7–8 minutes.
3. Add the green beans and simmer for another 3 minutes.
4. Break up the creamed coconut, add to the pan, and stir until it has melted and the sauce has thickened.
5. Scatter the chopped peanuts and mint on top and serve with rice.

Good food does not need to be complicated, and nor does it have to create a mountain of washing-up. This is our go-to one-pot pasta dish. With beautiful Mediterranean flavours and a sauce thickened with red lentils, all thrown into one pan, it really couldn't be tastier or easier.

ONE-POT MEDITERRANEAN LINGUINE

SERVES 4

500g passata
50g dried red lentils, rinsed
a splash of red wine
75g olives, halved
25g capers
75g sun-dried tomatoes,
    chopped
1 teaspoon dried chilli flakes
    (optional)
600ml vegetable stock
300g linguine
fresh basil, to serve

1. Put the passata, lentils and red wine into a large pan and bring to a simmer for 5 minutes, stirring every now and then to prevent the lentils sticking.
2. Add the olives, capers, sun-dried tomatoes, chilli flakes and stock, then return to the boil.
3. Add the linguine, and stir it into the sauce as it softens.
4. Cover the pan with a lid, then reduce the heat and allow the pasta to simmer for 10–12 minutes, until it is cooked to your preference. Stir intermittently to ensure the pasta does not stick, and add a little more water towards the end if you feel it needs it.
5. Sprinkle with fresh basil and serve.

It may be a 1970s classic, but quiche has never gone out of fashion with us. Instead of using egg, the vegan version uses tofu, which makes it protein-rich and every bit as tasty. Like its eggy counterpart, this quiche can be eaten warm or cold, so it makes a lovely light lunch or dinner, but it really comes into its own in picnic season.

QUICHE

SERVES 6–8

400g firm tofu (either plain or smoked)

1 pack of vegan shortcrust pastry (or you can make your own, using 175g plain flour and 85g vegan butter)

1 red onion, peeled and sliced

2 tablespoons olive or vegetable oil

1 garlic clove, peeled and minced or grated

1 red pepper, deseeded and sliced

½ courgette, thinly sliced

2 slices vegan bacon, chopped (optional)

a handful of spinach

2 tablespoons fresh parsley, finely chopped (or 2 teaspoons dried)

¼ teaspoon ground turmeric

2–3 tablespoons plant milk

150g vegan Cheddar-style cheese, grated

salt and pepper, to taste

1 large tomato, sliced

1. Press the tofu in a clean tea towel to remove as much of the water as possible, and set aside.
2. Roll out the pastry and line a 25cm tart tin with it, then pierce it all over with a fork and refrigerate for 30 minutes.
3. Heat the oven to 180°C fan/400°F/Gas Mark 6 and, when hot, bake the pastry case 'blind' (with nothing in it) for 15 minutes.
4. Meanwhile, fry the onion in the oil until soft, add the garlic, red pepper, courgette and vegan bacon (if using), and cook for another 3–5 minutes. Stir in the spinach and parsley until the spinach has just wilted, then set aside.
5. Put the tofu into a blender and pulse until it is crumbly. Add the turmeric and just a little plant milk, and blend again. Don't add too much milk, otherwise the quiche will be soggy. The mixture should be smooth but textured.
6. Mix the tofu with the vegetables, then stir in the grated cheese and season to taste.
7. Press the mixture into the part-baked pastry shell, and top with the sliced tomato.
8. Put the quiche back into the oven for 25–30 minutes, until the top has browned and the quiche is reasonably firm to touch. Let it stand for 15 minutes before slicing.

It's light, delicious and easy to make, but best of all, this dish just takes care of itself while you're outside enjoying the sun. The juices of the Mediterranean vegetables, the crispiness of the ciabatta and the fragrance of the fresh basil make this an ideal summer dish. Simply put it into the oven and come back when it's done.

BAKED SUMMER PANZANELLA

SERVES 4

750g medium tomatoes,
    quartered
2 red peppers, deseeded and
    roughly chopped
1 x 400g tin of cannellini beans,
    drained and rinsed
2 tablespoons olive oil
3 garlic cloves, peeled and
    minced or grated
200g ciabatta bread, roughly torn
salt and pepper, to taste
2 tablespoons red wine vinegar
2 teaspoons capers (optional)
a handful of fresh basil, torn

1. Heat the oven to 200°C fan/425°F/Gas Mark 7.
2. Put the tomatoes, peppers and cannellini beans into a roasting tray, and mix with the olive oil, crushed garlic and ciabatta. Season with salt and pepper and put into the oven for 25–30 minutes.
3. When the vegetables are softened, and the bread is crispy, remove from the oven.
4. Stir in the red wine vinegar and the capers (if using) and serve with the fresh basil scattered over the top.

This dish is very easy and very forgiving – you can tweak the amounts and it always comes out great! If you don't have pumpkin, use butternut squash, which looks very pretty when sliced into half-moon shapes. And you can add any vegetables, nuts or fruits you like to the couscous.

ROASTED PUMPKIN WITH MOROCCAN-STYLE COUSCOUS & COCONUT-LIME YOGHURT

SERVES 4

FOR THE PUMPKIN
750g pumpkin, peeled and cut
    into 2cm thick slices
3 tablespoons olive oil
2 tablespoons maple or agave
    syrup
2 teaspoons dried chipotle chilli
    flakes
1 teaspoon ground cumin
salt, to taste

FOR THE COUSCOUS
250g couscous (wholewheat or
    white)
175g shallots, peeled and finely
    diced
1 yellow pepper, deseeded and
    chopped
4 teaspoons ras el hanout
2 tablespoons olive oil
1 x 400g tin of chickpeas,
    drained and rinsed
35g flaked almonds
50g sultanas
salt and pepper, to taste
a handful of fresh parsley
1 lemon, juice only

FOR THE YOGHURT
200g coconut yoghurt
1 tablespoon agave syrup
2 limes, zest only
1 lime, juice only
1 tablespoon chopped fresh
    coriander (optional)

1. Heat the oven to 180°C fan/400°F/Gas Mark 6.
2. Place the pumpkin slices on a non-stick baking tray in a single layer.
3. In a jug or bowl, mix together the olive oil, maple or agave syrup, chilli flakes, cumin and salt. Drizzle this over the pumpkin and roast for 40 minutes.
4. About 10 minutes before the pumpkin is cooked, make the couscous. Put the grains into a large heatproof bowl and cover with boiling water. The water should come about ½cm above the couscous. Cover and set aside.
5. Gently fry the shallots, yellow pepper and ras el hanout in the olive oil until the shallots have softened – about 6–7 minutes.
6. Add the chickpeas, almonds and sultanas, and cook for another 2–3 minutes, stirring to ensure everything is coated in the spices. Season to taste.
7. Stir the vegetables into the couscous, combining well. Squeeze the lemon juice over the top and sprinkle over the parsley.
8. Finally, mix together all the yoghurt ingredients in a bowl.
9. When the pumpkin is soft, remove it from the oven and serve with the couscous. You can dollop the yoghurt on the side or drizzle it over the top.

Jackfruit has become a mainstay in the vegan world, as it shreds like pulled pork, and soaks up whatever flavours you team it with. It is a fruit, but it looks like meat and can be used on pizzas, and in chilli, nachos or tacos, though arguably it comes into its own when married with smoky barbecue flavours, packed inside a bun and topped with a crisp and tangy slaw. Stop drooling. Start cooking.

BARBECUED PULLED JACKFRUIT SANDWICH WITH SLAW

MAKES 2

1 x 400g tin of jackfruit in water
3 teaspoons barbecue seasoning
2 tablespoons olive oil
75g barbecue sauce
2 buns of your choice
a little vegan butter

FOR THE SLAW

50g celeriac, peeled
½ apple, cored
35g red cabbage
a squeeze of lemon juice
3 good tablespoons vegan
    mayonnaise
1 teaspoon Dijon mustard
1 tablespoon capers
a handful of fresh parsley,
    chopped

1. Drain and rinse the jackfruit, then cut out the hard core of the fruit and shred the rest with your fingers.
2. Mix well with the barbecue seasoning and 1 tablespoon of oil and set aside for at least 30 minutes.
3. Meanwhile, make the slaw. Grate or finely shred the celeriac, apple and red cabbage. Mix in the lemon juice, mayo, mustard, capers and parsley, and refrigerate until you need it.
4. Heat a non-stick frying pan and cook the jackfruit in the remaining 1 tablespoon of oil over a medium heat for about 5 minutes, stirring every now and then.
5. Stir in the barbecue sauce and cook for another 3–4 minutes.
6. Halve the buns and spread a little vegan butter on each of the cut sides. Divide the jackfruit between the two base halves, top with the slaw, and close each one with the other half of the bun to make two big beautiful messy sandwiches.

This is a hearty, tasty meal with all those earthy and warming flavours we love in a chilli. We have given this a fair-to-middling chilli kick, but if you prefer a milder assault on the taste buds, just halve the chilli and paprika. Possibly the best thing about this chilli is that the flavours develop and deepen over time. So, even if there are not four of you eating today, make a big pot anyway, and you'll have several dinners ready to go that will just get better and better. We particularly love it with nacho chips and guacamole.

ONE-POT THREE BEAN CHILLI

SERVES 4–6

2 tablespoons sunflower oil
1 large onion, peeled and diced
1 red pepper, deseeded and
    chopped
3 garlic cloves, peeled and
    minced or grated
2 teaspoons ground cumin
2 teaspoons paprika
2 teaspoons chilli powder
2 teaspoons dried oregano
2 teaspoons cacao powder (or
    cocoa powder)
250g sweet potatoes, peeled
    and chopped into roughly
    2.5cm chunks
3 x 400g tins of your choice of
    beans, drained and rinsed
2 x 400g tins of tomatoes
2 tablespoons tomato purée
300ml vegetable stock
2 tablespoons dark soy sauce
1 tablespoon vinegar (balsamic,
    red wine, apple cider,
    or whatever you have)
fresh coriander, chopped
    (optional)

1. Heat the oil in a large pan and fry the onion and red pepper for 7–8 minutes. Add the garlic, cumin, paprika, chilli powder, oregano and cacao, and cook for another 2 minutes, stirring to prevent sticking.

2. Add the sweet potatoes and beans and stir to coat them in the spices.

3. Add the tinned tomatoes, tomato purée, vegetable stock and soy sauce, then bring to the boil, stirring to prevent sticking. Cover with a lid, reduce the heat, and let it simmer for around 15 minutes, stirring every now and then.

4. When the sweet potatoes are tender, remove the pan from the heat and stir in the vinegar.

5. Serve, with some fresh coriander sprinkled over if you like.

Meat-free beef and traditional vegetables covered in a rich gravy make this a popular dish. Some people love the slight bitterness that a dark stout brings to this meal, but if that's not your jam, use a sweet brown ale instead. Or abandon the English pub classic for a French bistro special and use red wine, to make a vegan boeuf bourguignon-style pie. It's your pie. Do what you want with it. *See photo overleaf.*

'BEEF' & ALE PIE

SERVES 4

10g dried porcini mushrooms
1 large onion, peeled and diced
2 tablespoons sunflower oil
2 garlic cloves, peeled and
    minced or grated
2 carrots, peeled and diced
1 stick of celery, sliced
200g chestnut mushrooms,
    quartered
400g frozen vegan beef-style
    pieces
1 tablespoon dark brown sugar
1 tablespoon tomato purée
1 teaspoon wholegrain mustard
2 tablespoons red onion chutney
1 tablespoon chopped fresh
    parsley
½ teaspoon dried thyme
250ml vegan ale (or red wine if
    you prefer)
125ml vegetable stock
1 tablespoon cornflour, mixed
    with 3 tablespoons cold
    water
salt and pepper, to taste
150g ready-rolled puff pastry
a little plant milk

1. Cover the porcini mushrooms with boiling water and leave for 10 minutes. Chop the softened mushrooms into small pieces and set aside, reserving the liquid.

2. In a pan, gently fry the onion in the oil for 7–8 minutes, until softened. Add the garlic, carrots, celery, chestnut mushrooms and the porcini mushrooms. Fry for a further 5 minutes.

3. Add the vegan beef chunks and cook, stirring every now and then, for 5–6 minutes.

4. Add the sugar, tomato purée, mustard, chutney, parsley, thyme, ale, stock and 50ml of the porcini soaking water, and bring to the boil. Reduce the heat and let it simmer for 12–15 minutes, until the liquid has reduced.

5. Meanwhile, heat the oven to 200°C fan/425°F/Gas Mark 7.

6. When the stew is cooked, leave it simmering on the heat for a minute or two more while you stir in the cornflour mixture and allow the sauce to thicken. Then remove it from the heat and season with salt and pepper.

7. Pour the filling into one ovenproof dish, or four individual ones.

8. Cover with puff pastry and, if there are any leftover pastry scraps, cut out some decorative leaf shapes for the top of the pie.

9. Pierce the top of the pie with a fork in a couple of places to allow the steam to escape. Then brush the pastry with the plant milk, and bake the pie in the oven for 25–30 minutes, or until the pastry has risen and is golden.

Karahi refers to a type of pan with high sides commonly used in Indian cooking, but you can use any high-sided pan or wok. Yes, there are a lot of spices in this, but that's what makes it so outrageously tasty. It is a favourite in our Indian office, and the team suggests you serve it with chapati or another warm Indian bread to mop up those beautiful juices. You may also like to add a good dollop of coconut yoghurt and fresh mint to cool down that lovely chilli kick.

KARAHI MUSHROOMS

SERVES 2

1 large onion, roughly diced, plus 1 small onion, peeled and finely diced
1 large tomato, diced
2.5cm piece of fresh ginger, peeled and grated
2 garlic cloves, peeled
3 tablespoons sunflower oil
1 bay leaf
1 cinnamon stick
5 cardamom pods
3 cloves
½ teaspoon dried chilli flakes (less if you want less heat)
½ teaspoon salt
¼ teaspoon ground turmeric
½ teaspoon chilli powder
1 teaspoon ground coriander
2 teaspoons ground cumin
1 red pepper, deseeded and chopped into small pieces
250g mushrooms, sliced
¼ teaspoon garam masala
salt and pepper, to taste
1 teaspoon dried fenugreek leaves

1. First, make the base by blitzing the large onion, tomato, ginger and garlic in a blender. Set aside.
2. In a large pan, heat 2 tablespoons of the oil over a medium heat. Add the bay leaf, cinnamon stick, cardamom pods, cloves and chilli flakes, and fry for a minute.
3. Add the base from the blender to the pan, along with the salt. Increase the heat to bring it to a simmer, then reduce the heat and let it bubble away for 3–4 minutes.
4. Add the turmeric, chilli powder, ground coriander and cumin, and let it cook gently for 15 more minutes, stirring as needed to prevent it sticking. (The juiciness of your tomato will make a difference here.)
5. Meanwhile, in a separate pan, heat the remaining 1 tablespoon of oil and sauté the smaller onion, red pepper and mushrooms for about 8 minutes, until soft.
6. When the spicy base is ready, add the onions, peppers and mushrooms, along with the garam masala. Mix well and season to taste.
7. Add 125ml of water, cover the pan, bring to the boil, and let it simmer over a medium heat for 2–3 minutes. Add the dried fenugreek leaves and cook for 1 last minute.
8. Remove from the heat and serve with your choice of Indian bread such as roti or chapati, or rice.

This is a pie for potato lovers. It's a bit like a traditional shepherd's pie but the potato is layered top and bottom, with the 'meat' sandwiched in between. In its native land it's called *pastel de papa* or potato cake, and there are many variations on it. This vegan version, made with green olives and lentils, is the ultimate in comfort food.

ARGENTINIAN SHEPHERD'S PIE

SERVES 4

4 large potatoes, peeled and chopped
4 tablespoons sunflower oil
salt, to taste
1 tablespoon soy sauce
1 onion, peeled and chopped
1 red pepper, deseeded and chopped
1 teaspoon ground cumin
1 teaspoon paprika
1 teaspoon dried oregano
75g green olives, destoned and roughly chopped
1 x 400g tin of green lentils
50g vegan cheese, grated (optional, choose one that melts)

1. Boil the potatoes in a large pan of water until soft – usually around 15 minutes. Mash them with 2 tablespoons of the oil and some salt, then set aside.
2. Heat the oven to 200°C fan/425°F/Gas Mark 7.
3. In a dish, mix the soy sauce with 2 tablespoons of water. Set aside.
4. Fry the onion and pepper in a pan with the remaining 2 tablespoons of oil for 8–10 minutes, until the onion is soft. Add the cumin, paprika and oregano, and cook for another minute or two.
5. Stir in the olives, lentils and the soy sauce mix, and remove from the heat.
6. Layer half the mashed potatoes in the bottom of a baking dish (around 20 x 20cm). Spread the lentil mixture on top, and add the second layer of mashed potatoes on top of that.
7. Sprinkle with vegan cheese if you like, then bake in the oven for 20–25 minutes, or until it's browning on top.
8. Remove from the oven and serve.

This is adapted from a recipe donated exclusively to us by actor and Veganuary Ambassador, Soundarya Sharma. In Soundarya's version, dried chickpeas are soaked overnight, and it is cooked in a pressure cooker to create a traditional biryani, but we have speeded things up a bit and along the way it turned into chole chawal – lightly spiced chickpeas with rice. It does, however, retain those lovely original flavours and is every bit as satisfying. We absolutely love it, and we think you will, too. Thanks, Soundarya!

CHICKPEA CHOLE CHAWAL WITH RAITA

SERVES 4

FOR THE CHOLE CHAWAL
200g brown rice
2 tablespoons sunflower oil
1 star anise
1 small cinnamon stick
2 cardamom pods
4 black peppercorns
1 heaped teaspoon cumin seeds
2.5cm piece of fresh ginger,
    peeled and grated
1 large onion, peeled and finely
    sliced
½ teaspoon ground turmeric
½ teaspoon chilli powder
1 teaspoon ground coriander
salt and pepper, to taste
2 x 400g tins of chickpeas,
    drained and rinsed
1 large tomato, chopped

FOR THE RAITA
125g plain vegan yoghurt
65g cucumber, grated
20g onion, grated
¼ teaspoon cayenne
¼ teaspoon ground cumin
a handful of fresh mint leaves,
    finely chopped
2 tablespoons lemon juice
salt and pepper, to taste

TO SERVE (OPTIONAL)
fresh mint, chopped
fresh coriander, chopped
lemon wedges

1. First, soak the brown rice for 30 minutes, while you prepare the rest of the ingredients. Then drain.
2. In a large pan that has a lid, heat the oil over a medium heat.
3. Add the star anise, cinnamon stick, cardamom pods, peppercorns, cumin seeds and ginger, and sauté for 2 minutes.
4. Add the onion and cook for about 10–12 minutes, until it starts to brown. Remove a little of the onion and set it aside for the garnish.
5. Add the turmeric, chilli powder and ground coriander to the pan and cook for another minute or so, stirring. Then add the drained rice, some salt and 400ml of water.
6. Cover and bring to the boil, then reduce the heat and let it simmer for 15 minutes.
7. Add the chickpeas and another 240ml of water. Mix well, cover, and return to the boil, then reduce the heat and simmer for another 20 minutes, adding the tomato for the last 5 minutes.
8. Remove from the heat and remove the lid. The rice should be cooked and moist but not wet. Season to taste.
9. To make the raita, combine all the ingredients together in a bowl.
10. Serve the chole with the reserved caramelised onions, the raita and your chosen garnishes: mint, fresh coriander and/or lemon wedges.

Originally a Russian dish, stroganoff has found a fanbase all over the world, including in Brazil where this recipe comes from. It's a creamy stew with mustard as a key ingredient, and this version is really lovely. It's also what we call a hybrid meal. We're not making absolutely everything from scratch, but we have put enough effort into it that we can claim some bragging rights. Serve it with rice and fresh green vegetables for a lovely midweek meal.

BRAZILIAN AUBERGINE STROGANOFF

SERVES 4

2 medium aubergines, cut into bite-size pieces
2 teaspoons apple cider vinegar
2 tablespoons olive oil
3 garlic cloves, peeled and minced or grated
1 medium onion, peeled and chopped
1 green pepper, deseeded and chopped
salt, to taste
400g shop-bought pasta sauce (your choice)
2 tablespoons Dijon mustard
200ml oat milk

1. Put the chopped aubergines into a bowl of water with the vinegar and soak them for 10 minutes.
2. In a pan, heat the oil over a medium-high heat, add the garlic and onion, and sauté until golden – about 8–10 minutes.
3. Drain the aubergines. Add them to the pan along with the green pepper. Season with a little salt and let them cook for about 10 minutes until they have softened.
4. Add the pasta sauce, mustard and 100ml of water. Mix well and bring to the boil. Let it simmer for 3–4 minutes.
5. Finally, add the oat milk and adjust the salt. Let it simmer for a few minutes more to allow the sauce to thicken.
6. Serve with rice.

The national dish of Argentina, this hearty stew is typically meat-heavy, but in our version the flavour of vegetables can really shine through. We do give a little nod to its origins, though, and include some vegan chorizo, which gives it an authentic feel. So go ahead and serve yourself a big steaming bowl with some crusty bread and give thanks to our Latin American team for sharing this comfort-in-a-bowl with the world.

ARGENTINIAN LOCRO STEW

SERVES 4

275g vegan chorizo (or chorizo-flavoured vegan sausages)
2 tablespoons sunflower oil
1 onion, peeled and sliced
3 spring onions, chopped
½ red pepper, deseeded and diced
2 garlic cloves, peeled and minced or grated
2 tablespoons paprika
1 teaspoon smoked paprika
2 teaspoons ground cumin
2 tablespoons tomato purée
1 x 400g tin of butter beans, drained and rinsed
175g sweetcorn kernels (tinned or frozen)
375g pumpkin (or butternut squash), peeled, deseeded and cut into bite-size pieces
125g sweet potato, peeled and cut into bite-size pieces
½ courgette (or small yellow squash), chopped into bite-size pieces
325ml vegetable stock
salt and pepper, to taste
hot pepper sauce (optional, but absolutely recommended)

1. If the vegan chorizo you have bought requires cooking, do that now, then slice it and set it aside.
2. Heat the oil in a large saucepan and fry the onion, spring onion and red pepper for 6–7 minutes, until softening. Add the garlic, paprika, smoked paprika, cumin and tomato purée, and fry for another 2–3 minutes.
3. Add the butter beans, sweetcorn, pumpkin, sweet potatoes and courgettes and mix to coat them in the spices.
4. Add the vegetable stock, then cover with a lid and bring the stew to the boil. Reduce the heat and let it simmer for about 25 minutes, until the vegetables are nice and soft.
5. To thicken the sauce, mash some of the vegetables into it. Add the sliced vegan chorizo and season to taste, then let it warm for another minute or two. Season to taste.
6. Locro aficionados will add hot pepper sauce to serve, and we believe this really is the crowning glory of this meal.

It's quite a thrill to make a dish that tastes like it came from a restaurant when in fact you whipped it up yourself quite easily. Sshhhh. We won't tell if you don't. This is our take on the spicy, sticky, sweet sauces that always work so well with beancurd. We added fresh ginger juice because for us it's all about that zing, but be careful with that knobbly powerhouse. A little goes a long way.

STICKY GINGER SESAME TOFU

SERVES 2

400g firm tofu
5 tablespoons cornflour
1 teaspoon garlic powder
1 teaspoon salt
4 tablespoons sunflower oil
2 spring onions, finely sliced
2 garlic cloves, peeled and finely
    sliced
1–2 tablespoons sriracha sauce
2 tablespoons dark soy sauce
2 tablespoons maple syrup
4 tablespoons sugar
1 tablespoon toasted sesame oil
1 tablespoon grated fresh
    ginger, squeezed to get
    around ½ tablespoon of
    ginger juice

OPTIONAL GARNISHES

2 spring onions, cut diagonally
a handful of fresh coriander,
    chopped
a wedge of lime
sesame seeds

1. Drain the tofu and press it to remove as much of the liquid as possible. (If you don't have a tofu press, you can wrap it in a clean tea towel and place some books on top!) Then dice it.

2. Mix 3 tablespoons of the cornflour with the garlic powder and salt in a bowl and turn the tofu cubes over in it until they are coated. (This won't be perfect, but it doesn't need to be.)

3. Heat the oil in a frying pan and fry the tofu over a medium-high heat for 4–5 minutes on each side, until golden and crispy. Then remove from the pan and set aside.

4. Add the spring onions and garlic to the same pan, and fry for a minute or two. Then add the sriracha sauce, soy sauce, maple syrup, sugar and 220ml of water, and bring to a simmer.

5. In a small bowl, mix the last two 2 tablespoons of cornflour with a little water to form a smooth paste, and stir it into the liquid to thicken it.

6. Stir in the toasted sesame oil and ginger juice, then pour the sticky sweet and spicy sauce over the tofu.

7. Serve with rice and garnish with more spring onions, chopped coriander, a wedge of lime and/or a sprinkle of sesame seeds.

Dal is a thing of wonder. It's full of protein, cheap to make, and so tasty, too, which is why we were keen to include a recipe from our Indian team. And it looked delicious! However, it contained some ingredients that are commonly found in India but are much harder to find here. So we bring you a version you can whip up using what's in your cupboard, making it an 'every day dal'. It's so filling, warming and satisfying we think it really is good enough to eat every day! We love it with rice or roti, and we hope you love it, too.

EVERY DAY DAL

SERVES 4

4 tablespoons sunflower oil
1 large onion, peeled and diced
2 garlic cloves, peeled and minced or grated
1 teaspoon ground turmeric
1 teaspoon dried chilli flakes
2.5cm piece of fresh ginger, peeled and grated
1 litre salted water or vegetable stock
250g split red lentils, rinsed (see note below on using whole red lentils)
300g sweet potatoes, peeled and cut into 2cm pieces
1 x 400g tin of kidney beans, drained and rinsed
100g spinach leaves
salt and pepper, to taste
fresh coriander, to serve (optional)

1. Heat the oil in a pan and fry the onion over a medium heat until softened and starting to brown – about 10–12 minutes, stirring every now and then to prevent the onions sticking.

2. Add the garlic, turmeric, chilli flakes and ginger and fry for another 3 minutes, again stirring to prevent sticking. Set aside.

3. Meanwhile, bring the salted water or stock to the boil. Add the lentils and bring back to the boil. Remove any froth from the top with a spoon, then add the sweet potatoes and kidney beans. Place a lid on the pan and let it simmer for 10 minutes.

4. When the lentils and sweet potatoes are soft, remove the pan from the heat and drain partially. Retain just enough liquid so it has the consistency of a thick sauce (or retain more water if you prefer your dal more soupy).

5. Stir in the cooked onions and spices.

6. Return the pan to the hot stove top, add the spinach, and stir until it has wilted.

7. Season to taste and serve, garnished with fresh coriander if you like.

Note: If you use *whole* red lentils instead of *split* red lentils, that's completely fine but they do take a little longer to cook. Boil them for 10 minutes before you add the sweet potatoes and kidney beans, then follow the rest of the recipe.

This absolutely delicious and very satisfying stew is perfect for an autumn or winter evening. It is also a very forgiving recipe. Use the veggies you have in the cupboard; add whatever beans you like. Leave out the spices if you want, or add fresh herbs at the end. To make the flavours even deeper, substitute 200ml of the stock with cider or red wine. Don't worry too much over the size of the vegetables or the exact cooking time. If the veggies are soft, dinner is ready!

ONE-POT BUTTER BEAN & ROOT VEG STEW WITH CHEESY DUMPLINGS

SERVES 4

FOR THE DUMPLINGS
60g vegan butter
125g self-raising flour
60g vegan cheese, grated
¼ tsp black pepper

FOR THE STEW
2 tablespoons olive oil
1 red onion, peeled and chopped
1 stick of celery, finely sliced
2 garlic cloves, peeled and
    minced or grated
1 teaspoon paprika
½ teaspoon chilli powder
850g root vegetables (such as
    parsnips, potatoes, celeriac,
    carrots, squash, sweet
    potatoes), roughly cut into
    bite-size chunks
600ml vegetable stock (make
    it just a little stronger than the
    packet recommendation)
1 bay leaf
1 x 400g tin of butter beans,
    drained and rinsed
1 tablespoon tomato purée
1 tablespoon peanut butter
1 tablespoon vegetable gravy
    granules

1. To make the dumplings, rub the vegan butter into the flour with your fingertips until it looks like fine breadcrumbs. Mix in the grated cheese and black pepper and add 1 tablespoon of cold water.

2. Using your hands, gently bring the mixture together to form a dough, being careful not to squeeze it or overwork it. If it's too crumbly, add another ½ tablespoon of water. Now, form 12 small balls with your hands, working the dumplings as little as possible. Set aside.

3. In a large saucepan, heat the oil and gently fry the onion and celery over a medium heat for 8–10 minutes, until soft. Add the garlic, paprika and chilli powder and fry for 2 minutes more.

4. Add the chopped vegetables and stir to coat them in the spices, then add the stock and the bay leaf. Cover with a lid and bring to the boil, then reduce the heat and simmer for 5 minutes.

5. Stir in the butter beans, tomato purée and peanut butter. Then, while it's still simmering, stir in the gravy granules. The sauce should thicken.

6. Pop the 12 dumplings on top, giving them each space to grow, then put the lid back on and let the stew simmer gently for another 15 minutes. About halfway through, push a wooden spoon down the side of the pan and gently lift the stew to ensure it stays moist at the bottom and does not stick. Repeat this round the pan, being sure not to disturb the dumplings, then replace the lid.

7. After 15 minutes, test the vegetables with a knife to ensure they're soft, and give them a few more minutes if they need it. By now, the dumplings should be fluffy.

8. Serve the stew with the dumplings.

This simple one-pot dish is full of flavour and is hearty enough to fill you right up. It's based on the much-loved Greek *patates yahni*, or potato stew, but with added aubergines and olives. Delicious! And here's our favourite cheat: instead of passata, a tin of vegan tomato soup works really well. So make yourself a big, beautiful bowlful, and go right ahead and mop up those juices with some fresh bread if that takes your fancy.

ONE-POT GREEK-STYLE AUBERGINE AND POTATO STEW

SERVES 4

4 tablespoons olive oil
1 red onion, peeled and sliced
2 garlic cloves, peeled and
    minced or grated
2 aubergines, roughly diced
750g potatoes, peeled and diced
    (around 3cm)
400g passata
1 tablespoon tomato purée
1 bay leaf
1 teaspoon dried oregano
350ml vegetable stock
black pepper, to taste
75g olives, your choice of green
    or black, pitted and halved
a handful of fresh parsley,
    chopped (optional)

1. In a large saucepan, heat the oil over a medium heat and fry the onion until softening – about 7–8 minutes. Add the garlic and cook for another minute or two.
2. Add the aubergines and potatoes, stir well, then add the passata, tomato purée, bay leaf, oregano and stock. Season with black pepper.
3. Cover with a lid and bring to the boil, then reduce the heat and let the stew simmer for 30–35 minutes.
4. When the potatoes are lovely and soft, remove from the heat and stir in the olives. Sprinkle the parsley over the top to serve.

This traditional-made vegan recipe comes courtesy of our German team. It has the characteristic slightly sour, gently spiced, umami flavours that goulash lovers expect, and it works perfectly with the super creamy mashed potato. Experienced cooks will be able to cook both the goulash and potatoes at the same time, but the easiest way for new cooks to make this is to cook the goulash first, and while it's simmering away, start making the potatoes. Then you can just put the goulash back on the hob to heat through.

GOULASH WITH MASHED POTATOES

SERVES 4

FOR THE GOULASH

4 tablespoons sunflower oil
400g smoked tofu, drained and
    cubed
200g plain tofu, drained and
    cubed
2 large onions, peeled and diced
2 garlic cloves, peeled and
    minced or grated
4 tablespoons tomato purée
a pinch of sugar
2 red peppers, deseeded and
    chopped into strips
2 teaspoons smoked paprika
2 teaspoons hot paprika
200ml red wine
300ml vegetable stock
1 bay leaf
4 tablespoons soy sauce
salt and pepper, to taste

FOR THE MASHED POTATO

1.2kg floury potatoes, peeled and
    cut into chunks
2 tablespoons vegan butter
200ml vegan cream
200ml plant milk
salt and pepper, to taste
½ teaspoon freshly grated
    nutmeg

1. Heat 2 tablespoons of oil in a large pan and sear the tofu on all sides. Remove from the pan and set aside.

2. Heat the remaining 2 tablespoons of oil in the pan and sauté the onions over a medium heat until translucent (about 8–10 minutes), then add the garlic and cook for another minute or two.

3. Add the tomato purée and fry a little, adding a pinch of sugar.

4. Add the red peppers, smoked paprika and hot paprika, and fry for 3–4 minutes, stirring every now and then.

5. Stir in the wine and stock, add the bay leaf, and bring to the boil. Turn down the heat and let it simmer for about 6–8 minutes, until you have a nice thick sauce.

6. Meanwhile, cook the potatoes in boiling salted water for about 20 minutes. Drain and leave to cool slightly, then mash them.

7. Melt the vegan butter in a pan. Add the vegan cream and plant milk, bring to the boil, then mix into the mashed potato. Season with salt, pepper and the freshly grated nutmeg.

8. Add the tofu and soy sauce to the goulash and let it warm through. Remove the bay leaf and season to taste.

9. Serve the goulash with the mashed potato.

This deliciously versatile one-pot meal is perfect for a quick midweek dinner. You can substitute any dense vegetable for the potatoes, and swap mushrooms or courgettes for the pepper, green beans or butternut squash for the cauliflower, and any tinned beans for the chickpeas. So this recipe is, in fact, dozens of different recipes. We just happened to have potatoes and cauliflower, but whatever is in your cupboards and freezer is what's for dinner. Why make things more complicated than they need to be?

ONE-POT STORE CUPBOARD CURRY

SERVES 4

2 tablespoons sunflower oil
1 large onion, peeled and diced
1 yellow pepper, deseeded and
    roughly chopped
2 garlic cloves, peeled and
    minced or grated
2 tablespoons curry powder
500g potatoes, peeled and diced
    into roughly 4cm pieces
500ml vegetable stock
300g cauliflower, cut into florets
1 x 400g tin of chickpeas,
    drained and rinsed
75g creamed coconut, broken
    into small pieces
100g spinach leaves, fresh or
    frozen

1. In a large pan, heat the oil and fry the onion and yellow pepper for about 7–8 minutes. Add the garlic and curry powder and cook for another minute or two.

2. Add the potatoes and stir to cover them with the spices, then add the stock.

3. Bring to the boil, cover with a lid, then reduce the heat and simmer for 5–6 minutes.

4. Add the cauliflower and chickpeas, cover again, then return to the boil and simmer for another 5–6 minutes, until the cauliflower and potatoes are both tender.

5. Turn off the heat but leave the pan on the hob as you stir in the creamed coconut, which will thicken up the sauce as it melts into it. (If it becomes too thick, just add a little more water or stock.) Finally, stir in the spinach until it has just wilted.

6. That's it. Your dinner is ready. Serve it as it is or with rice or bread.

3.

SNACKS &
LIGHT MEALS

If you were around in the 1980s, you would have put anything and everything between two slices of bread and toasted it in your sandwich maker. Times have changed, but the joy of a delicious gooey filling oozing out between slices of golden toasted bread is timeless. You don't need a sandwich maker to make these, but if you still have one, dust it off and give it a try for this super tasty snack.

CHICKPEA 'TUNA' MELT

MAKES 2 SANDWICHES

125g tinned chickpeas, drained
½ small red onion, peeled and
    finely chopped
½ stick of celery, finely diced
50g tinned sweetcorn, drained
2–3 tablespoons vegan
    mayonnaise
2 teaspoons capers
½ teaspoon Dijon mustard
½ tablespoon fresh dill, chopped
    (or ½ teaspoon dried)
salt and pepper, to taste
a little vegan butter
4 slices of bread (wholemeal or
    white)
25g vegan cheese, grated
    (choose one that melts)

1. In a bowl, mash the chickpeas with a fork until they are broken down.
2. Add the onion, celery, sweetcorn, vegan mayo, capers, mustard and dill, and season to taste.
3. Spread vegan butter on one side of each of the 4 slices of bread.
4. On the dry side of 2 slices, spread the chickpea mixture and top with the grated cheese. Place the second piece of bread on top to close the sandwiches, with the butter on the outside.
5. If you have a toasted sandwich maker, heat it up and cook the sandwiches until nicely browned.
6. If you don't, heat a frying pan or griddle pan over a medium heat. Fry each sandwich with the buttered side of the bread facing down for 4–5 minutes, until the base is golden, then turn over carefully with a spatula and cook for another 3–4 minutes.
7. Eat it while it's warm and gooey.

Cheese sauce has a reputation for being difficult to make: lose focus for even a moment and it will go lumpy or stick or burn, or, if you are unlucky, all three. And it's true that there is one stage of the recipe (step 5) where continuous stirring is needed, but this recipe makes the process pretty simple, and the result is a batch of cute cheesy tartlets that are perfect for picnics, lunchboxes or snacks. Kids *really* love them.

CHEESY LEEK & SWEETCORN TARTLETS

MAKES 12–15 TARTLETS

1 small leek, cleaned and very finely sliced
1 tablespoon olive oil
40g vegan butter
75g sweetcorn (tinned or frozen and defrosted)
1½ tablespoons plain flour
175ml unsweetened plant milk
50g vegan Cheddar-style cheese, grated (choose one that melts)
salt and black pepper, to taste
1 sheet of ready-rolled vegan shortcrust pastry

1. Heat the oven to 180°C fan/400°F/Gas Mark 6.
2. Fry the leek in the olive oil and 10g of the vegan butter for a few minutes, until it has softened. Add the sweetcorn and set aside.
3. To make the cheese sauce, melt the remaining 30g of vegan butter in a saucepan over a medium heat. When it has melted, add the flour and keep stirring for a couple more minutes while on the heat. It should form a smooth, thick paste.
4. Now, remove it from the heat while you add the plant milk, a little at a time, stirring until it is all combined and smooth.
5. This is the bit where you need to focus. Ready? Return the pan to the heat, and bring to the boil slowly, stirring all the while to make sure no lumps form. By the time it comes to the boil, it should have thickened into a lovely creamy sauce.
6. As soon as it boils, remove the pan from the heat and add the cheese, stirring until it melts into the sauce. Stir in the leeks and sweetcorn, then season to taste. Set aside.
7. Using a pastry cutter, cut out the cases for the tartlets and put them into the holes of a cupcake baking tray. Spoon in the mixture (not quite up to the rim, as it will spill over) and bake for 18–20 minutes, until the filling has just started to brown.
8. Remove from the oven and cool on a wire rack before serving.

Note: This is home cooking at its finest, and these tartlets are what you might call 'rustic'. If you like beautiful presentation, a sprinkle of finely chopped fresh parsley over the top works wonders.

Deliciously messy to eat, this creamy, sweet and gently spiced sandwich is best when made with fresh seeded crusty bread. These are large portions, because no one likes a stingy sandwich. Don't forget to wear a bib.

CORONATION CHICKPEA SANDWICH

SERVES 2

30g sultanas
1 medium red onion, peeled and
 finely chopped
1 tablespoon sunflower oil
1 x 400g tin of chickpeas,
 drained and rinsed
1 garlic clove, peeled and
 minced or grated
2 teaspoons curry powder
¼ teaspoon ground ginger
75g mayonnaise
75g natural soya yoghurt
1 tablespoon mango chutney
a handful of fresh coriander or
 parsley, chopped
salt and pepper, to taste
4 slices of bread, or 2 slices if
 serving as an open sandwich
watercress, or other salad leaves,
 to serve

1. Soak the sultanas in hot water for 10 minutes, then drain and set aside.
2. Fry the onion gently in the oil until it is soft – about 6–8 minutes.
3. Add the chickpeas, garlic, curry powder and ginger, and cook for another 4–5 minutes, stirring every now and then.
4. Stir in the sultanas, then remove the pan from the heat and let the mixture cool.
5. Lightly mash the chickpeas so that some are crushed and some remain whole. Stir in the mayo, yoghurt, mango chutney, and the fresh coriander or parsley. Season to taste.
6. Serve in a sandwich with watercress or other salad leaves.

This is a quick, tasty, healthy recipe that is really easy to make. If you don't have fresh green beans, use frozen and just reduce the cooking time a bit. We love this as a meal in itself with rice or fresh bread to mop up those juices, but it is also a great side dish and a barbecue favourite. Best of all, it's one recipe where overcooking the vegetables may just make it better!

GREEN BEANS WITH CARAWAY

SERVES 4

1 medium onion, finely diced
2 tablespoons olive oil
2 garlic cloves, peeled and
  minced or grated
1 teaspoon caraway seeds
½–1 teaspoon dried chilli flakes
1 x 400g tin of tomatoes
125ml vegetable stock
400g green beans, topped and
  tailed
black pepper, to taste

1. Fry the onion in the oil over a medium heat until softening – about 7–8 minutes – then add the garlic and fry for another minute or two.
2. Add the caraway seeds and the chilli flakes and cook for another minute.
3. Stir in the tinned tomatoes, vegetable stock and beans, and season with black pepper.
4. Bring to the boil, then cover, reduce the heat and simmer for 10–15 minutes, depending on whether you like your vegetables with a crunch still, or soft and deliciously stewed. This recipe suits both. Frozen beans contain more water, so if you are using them, you may need to remove the lid for the last 3 or 4 minutes of cooking to help thicken up the sauce.
5. Serve as a side dish or in a big bowl with a big hunk of bread.

These make a lovely change from the usual veggie sausagemeat-filled rolls and are a great way to get your kids (or yourself) to eat more plants. They're perfect for lunchboxes, picnics, to go with salads, or just as a snack. If you can't find vegan feta, just use any vegan cheese.

WALNUT, ROSEMARY & FETA ROLLS

SERVES 4–6

125g walnuts
1 tablespoon olive oil
1 small leek, cleaned and finely sliced
½ red pepper, deseeded and finely diced
1 garlic clove, peeled and minced or grated
1 sprig of fresh rosemary, finely chopped (or ½ teaspoon dried rosemary)
1 tablespoon tomato purée
100g vegan feta cheese, broken into small pieces
salt and pepper, to taste
1 sheet of ready-rolled vegan puff pastry
1 tablespoon plant milk
2 tablespoons sesame seeds (optional)

1. Heat the oven to 200°C fan/425°F/Gas Mark 7.
2. Toast the walnuts by frying them in a dry pan over a medium-high heat, turning them over, until they are golden – about 5 minutes. When cool enough to handle, break them into small pieces.
3. Heat the olive oil in a pan and fry the leek, red pepper and garlic until soft – about 5 minutes.
4. Add the walnuts, and stir in the rosemary, tomato purée and feta. Season to taste. Let it cool completely, as it will be easier to shape the rolls and they will hold together better.
5. Cut your pastry sheet into three large rectangles and mould the filling into a sausage shape down the middle of each. Press the filling together as you bring up the sides of the pastry to meet. Press the pastry edges together, then turn each roll over and cut them in half or into smaller pieces if you prefer, pushing any spilled stuffing back inside.
6. Brush each piece with a little plant milk and sprinkle sesame seeds on top (if using).
7. Line a baking sheet with baking parchment and place the rolls on it, with the join facing downwards. Cook for 20–25 minutes, until golden brown.
8. Remove from the oven and allow to cool before eating.

Warning! These cauliflower wings are SPICY, but they taste so good and the refreshing creamy dip counters some of that delicious heat. These are one of our favourite finger foods, and we're confident they'll soon be one of yours, too.

BUFFALO WINGS WITH CREAMY DILL DIP

SERVES 4

FOR THE WINGS
180ml plant milk
120g plain flour
1 tablespoon garlic powder
1 tablespoon onion powder
½ teaspoon salt
1 large cauliflower, broken into
    florets
1 tablespoon vegan butter
200g hot pepper sauce

FOR THE CREAMY DILL DIP
100g vegan mayonnaise
100g vegan crème fraîche
½ tablespoon fresh dill, finely
    chopped
½ tablespoon fresh parsley, finely
    chopped
½ tablespoon fresh chives, finely
    chopped
¼ teaspoon onion powder
¼ teaspoon garlic powder
salt and pepper, to taste

1. Heat the oven to 220°C fan/475°F/Gas Mark 9.
2. In a large bowl, whisk together the milk, flour, garlic powder, onion powder and salt until well combined into a batter.
3. Add the cauliflower to the bowl and turn the pieces over to coat them in the batter.
4. Place each piece on a baking tray lined with baking parchment, making sure the florets are not touching each other. Put them into the oven for 15 minutes, removing them after 7 minutes to turn them over.
5. While they are cooking, melt the vegan butter and mix it with the hot pepper sauce.
6. Toss the now part-cooked cauliflower in the sauce, then put back into the oven for another 20 minutes until it is crispy.
7. Meanwhile, to make the creamy dill dip, whisk together the mayo and crème fraîche, then stir in all the other ingredients and season to taste. Refrigerate until ready to use, and serve with the hot wings.

These flatbreads are cheap and easy to make, but as the dough needs an hour to rise, they are a bit time-consuming. If you like the idea but cannot wait, here's our cheat's version: use shop-bought pitta breads for the base. And if you want to get fancy, try using bruschetta topping or olive tapenade instead of the sun-dried tomato purée.

FLATBREAD PIZZAS

MAKES 4 PIZZAS

250g strong white flour, plus a
    little more for dusting
1 teaspoon salt
1 teaspoon fast-action dried
    yeast
160ml lukewarm water
2 teaspoons olive oil, plus a little
    more for oiling the bowl
8 tablespoons sun-dried tomato
    purée
your choice of toppings:
    tomatoes, peppers, red
    onions, pineapple,
    capers, olives, vegan
    sausage, pine nuts, spinach,
    mushrooms, sweetcorn,
    jalapeños
100g vegan cheese, grated
    (choose one that melts)

1. In a large bowl, combine the flour, salt and yeast.
2. Put the water and oil into a separate bowl or jug, then pour these wet ingredients into the dry ones, mixing well.
3. Use your hands to gently bring together the dough. Turn it out on to a lightly floured surface and knead it for 5–10 minutes, until it is soft and smooth.
4. Lightly oil a bowl and place the dough inside. Cover it with a clean tea towel and leave for an hour, or until it has doubled in size.
5. Now, heat the oven to 220°C fan/475°F/Gas Mark 9, and put a baking tray in to heat up.
6. Divide the dough into four equal parts. With your hands, roll each piece into a ball. Then use a rolling pin to roll each ball out into an oval shape about 20cm long.
7. Carefully dust the heated baking tray with a little more flour, then place the flatbreads on the tray and put them into the oven for 4–5 minutes.
8. Take the breads out of the oven – they will have puffed up a bit – and cover them with the sun-dried tomato purée, your choice of toppings and the vegan cheese. Return to the oven for 8–10 minutes, or until the edges are just starting to brown.
9. Serve straight away.

We love these simple, spicy fritters just as they are, but when eaten with a drizzle of the sweet chilli sauce, we're talking about a whole new level of sublime. Dial down the heat a little and kids are sure to love them, too.

SWEETCORN FRITTERS WITH SWEET CHILLI SAUCE

SERVES 4

FOR THE SWEET CHILLI SAUCE
1 tablespoon cornflour
100ml rice wine vinegar
50ml water
175g caster sugar
2 red chillies, finely chopped
3cm piece of fresh ginger, peeled and grated
1 garlic clove, peeled and finely minced or grated
1 tablespoon dark soy sauce
1 tablespoon tomato ketchup
½ teaspoon salt

FOR THE FRITTERS
3 tablespoons ground flax seeds
120g plain flour
2 teaspoons baking powder
1–2 teaspoons dried chilli flakes (optional)
225ml plant milk
200g frozen or canned sweetcorn kernels, drained
6 spring onions, thinly sliced
a handful of fresh coriander, roughly chopped
salt and pepper, to taste
oil, for frying

1. First, make the sweet chilli sauce. Mix the cornflour with 2 tablespoons of water and set aside.
2. Put the rest of the chilli sauce ingredients into a saucepan and bring to the boil. Reduce the heat, simmer for 5 minutes, then stir in the cornflour and water mix.
3. Let it bubble away for another 5 minutes until it has thickened, stirring every now and then. Remove from the heat and set it aside to cool.
4. In a small bowl, combine the flax seeds with 6 tablespoons of warm water and set aside for 5 minutes.
5. In a separate larger bowl, mix the flour, baking powder and the chilli flakes (if using).
6. Stir in the plant milk and the flax seed mixture, and mix well to form a batter.
7. Add the sweetcorn, spring onions and fresh coriander. Season to taste.
8. We're ready to fry! Heat the oil in a non-stick frying pan over a medium-high heat. When the oil is hot, drop in a tablespoon of the fritter mixture at a time, and cook for around 3 minutes on each side, or until browned.
9. Drain on kitchen paper and serve with the chilli sauce as a dip on the side or drizzled over the top to serve.

A note on chillies: The standard chillies available in supermarkets often have little heat. If you prefer more, try finger or bird's-eye chillies, and if you want still more, leave the seeds in! If you like less heat, use fewer or milder chillies.

For a light summer meal, this is hard to beat. Bursting with fresh flavours, and drizzled with creamy tahini, this is surely the nicest way to eat your greens.

CITRUS SUMMER GREENS WITH TAHINI LIME DRIZZLE

SERVES 2, OR 4 AS A SIDE

FOR THE SUMMER GREENS
250g asparagus, woody ends discarded
200g tenderstem broccoli
200g green beans, topped and tailed
3 tablespoons olive oil
salt and pepper, to taste
1 lemon, zest only

FOR THE TAHINI LIME DRIZZLE
1 teaspoon agave syrup
2 limes, juice and zest
70g tahini
¼ teaspoon salt

1. Heat the oven to 200°C fan/425°F/Gas Mark 7.
2. Place the vegetables on a roasting tray, drizzle with the oil, and season with salt and pepper.
3. Roast for 20 minutes, until the vegetables have softened, stirring them halfway through.
4. Meanwhile, to make the tahini sauce, mix the agave, lime juice and zest into the tahini and season with salt. Add enough water to get your preferred consistency.
5. Sprinkle the vegetables with the lemon zest and drizzle the tahini sauce over them to serve.

This is a super tasty way to get loads of veggies into your meal, and you can adapt it depending on what you have in the refrigerator. But it's the garlicky cream cheese that really makes this lunchtime wrap so very good. This is a gift from our US office, and we are VERY grateful for it!

VEGGIE WRAPS

SERVES 4

FOR THE FILLING
2 tablespoons olive oil
1 onion, peeled and diced
2 garlic cloves, peeled and
    minced or grated
1 courgette, diced
2 roasted red peppers
    (from a jar), chopped
200g mushrooms, sliced
salt and pepper, to taste

FOR THE CREAM CHEESE
100g plain vegan cream cheese
2 tablespoons lemon juice
1 garlic clove, peeled and
    minced or grated
1 teaspoon dried chilli flakes

TO SERVE
4 tortilla wraps
a handful of spinach leaves
100g tomatoes, diced

1. Start by making the filling. Heat the olive oil in a large pan and sauté the onion for 4–5 minutes, until softening.
2. Add the garlic, courgette, roasted red peppers and mushrooms, and cook for about 15 more minutes, stirring every now and then. Season to taste.
3. While the vegetables are cooking, mix the vegan cream cheese with the lemon juice, garlic and chilli flakes in a bowl.
4. To serve, heat the tortillas in a dry pan over a medium heat for a minute or so. Spread a thin layer of the cream cheese over each one, add a handful of spinach, then add the veggies. Top with fresh tomatoes and roll up the wrap.
5. Heat in the hot dry pan for 1–2 minutes on each side, then cut diagonally in half.
6. Eat as it is or serve it – as our friends in the US do – with fries.

This tasty warm salad bowl is both filling and healthy, which makes it a winner all round. But perhaps the most beautiful thing about it is that it is also highly adaptable. Want to add tofu or beans? Go ahead! Got carrots to use up? Chuck them into the oven too! You'd like to try it with spicy peanut sauce instead of a zingy dressing? Be our guest!

ROASTED VEGGIE & GRAIN BOWL

SERVES 4

FOR THE BOWL
450g sweet potatoes, peeled and cut into small cubes (about 2cm)
2 red onions, peeled and sliced
1 tablespoon olive oil
salt and pepper, to taste
275g easy-cook brown rice, rinsed
125g quinoa
80g kale, shredded and tough stalks discarded
4 apples, cored and sliced
100g roasted and salted almonds, roughly chopped

FOR THE DRESSING
100g plain vegan yoghurt
50ml balsamic vinegar
1 teaspoon Dijon mustard
1 teaspoon maple syrup
½ lemon, juice only
salt and pepper, to taste
2 tablespoons olive oil

1. Heat the oven to 220°C fan/475°F/Gas Mark 9.
2. In a large bowl, mix the sweet potato cubes and onion slices (plus any other vegetables you may wish to add) with the oil and season to taste. Transfer to a large baking sheet and roast in the oven for 25–30 minutes, stirring halfway through.
3. In a large pot, combine the brown rice and quinoa with 850ml of water and bring to the boil. Cover and cook for 20 minutes, checking towards the end to make sure it has not dried out completely. Remove from the heat and let it sit for another 20 minutes. The water should have been absorbed, leaving the grains nice and fluffy.
4. Combine all the dressing ingredients, except the olive oil, in a small bowl. Then slowly add the olive oil while whisking the dressing.
5. Put the grains into a bowl and add the roasted veg, kale, apple and almonds, then add the dressing, stirring to combine everything well.

4.

SALADS

This recipe was gifted to us by our US office, and since Caesar salad is practically their national dish, we had to include it. The slightly smoky flavour of the lettuce with the sweetness of the maple syrup and the tanginess of the dressing makes a memorable – and very tasty – combination. Lots of supermarkets sell 'bacon bits', which are often vegan and make a fantastic addition to this already lovely dish.

GRILLED CAESAR SALAD

SERVES 2 AS A LIGHT MEAL, 4 AS A STARTER OR SIDE

FOR THE SALAD
60ml olive oil, plus 2 tablespoons for grilling
1 tablespoon maple syrup
salt and pepper, to taste
100g bread, cut into roughly 2cm cubes
2 heads of romaine lettuce
30g vegan parmesan

FOR THE DRESSING
100g vegan mayonnaise
½ lemon, juice only
2 tablespoons nutritional yeast
1 tablespoon Dijon mustard
1 tablespoon capers
½–1 garlic clove, peeled and minced or grated
salt and pepper, to taste

1. Heat the oven to 170°C fan/375°F/Gas Mark 5.
2. In a large bowl, whisk together the 60ml of olive oil and the maple syrup, then season with salt and pepper.
3. Toss the cubes of bread in this mixture, then spread them evenly on a baking sheet and bake for 25 minutes, turning them halfway through. Remove from the oven and set aside.
4. Heat the grill to medium-high. Slice each head of romaine in half lengthways from root to tip. Brush the cut sides with olive oil and sprinkle with salt and pepper. Place them under the hot grill, cut side up, and grill until the lettuce has a light char. Remove carefully (they're hot!), let them cool, then roughly chop.
5. Whisk together all the dressing ingredients in a bowl. You can thin it out with a little water if necessary.
6. To serve, place the chopped lettuce on a platter and sprinkle the croutons, dressing and vegan parmesan over the top.

This Texan favourite is a salsa-style salad, made from beans and corn, with fresh lime dressing. It couldn't be easier to make, and is great for barbecues and picnics, or when a large number of people drop by unexpectedly! Serve it with tortilla chips for scooping.

COWBOY CAVIAR

SERVES 6–8

FOR THE SALSA
1 x 400g tin of black beans, drained and rinsed
1 x 400g tin of black-eyed beans, drained and rinsed
1 x 400g tin of sweetcorn, drained and rinsed
¼ red onion, peeled and finely chopped
1 red pepper, deseeded and chopped
15 cherry tomatoes, quartered
1 fresh green chilli, finely diced (optional)

FOR THE DRESSING
30ml olive oil
2 limes, juice only
1 teaspoon agave syrup
1 garlic clove, peeled and grated
salt and pepper, to taste

1. Mix the beans and corn in a large bowl. Add the chopped onion, red pepper, tomatoes and the chilli (if using).
2. In a mason jar or bowl, mix together all the dressing ingredients.
3. Pour the dressing over the bean and veggie mixture, stir well and serve.

A note on chillies: The standard chillies available in supermarkets often have little heat. If you prefer more, try finger or bird's-eye chillies, and if you want still more, leave the seeds in! If you like less heat, use fewer or milder chillies.

Ceviche is a Latin American seafood salad, but this version, which uses hearts of palm, has all the same flavour, texture and zing. It's a lovely summertime dish, and we think it comes into its own when served with tortilla chips, flatbreads or rice cakes. Hearts of palm can be found in tins in many supermarkets, making this simple dish a big hit.

HEARTS OF PALM CEVICHE

SERVES 4

1 x 400g tin of hearts of palm,
    drained and rinsed
2 medium tomatoes, diced
1 avocado, peeled, stone
    removed and sliced
½ yellow pepper, deseeded and
    finely chopped
¼ cucumber, diced
4 spring onions, sliced
1 green chilli pepper, finely diced
    (optional)
20g fresh coriander, finely
    chopped
3 tablespoons olive oil
1 lime, juice only
salt and pepper, to taste

1. Drain and rinse the hearts of palm and place them in a medium-sized bowl. Using two forks, shred them finely.
2. Add all the vegetables and the coriander to the bowl. Stir gently to combine.
3. Add the olive oil, lime juice, salt and pepper and stir again. Then refrigerate for at least 30 minutes to allow all the flavours to combine.
4. Now, it's time to eat.

A note on chillies: The standard chillies available in supermarkets often have little heat. If you prefer more, try finger or bird's-eye chillies, and if you want still more, leave the seeds in! If you like less heat, use fewer or milder chillies.

Normally made with bulgur wheat, we have instead made this classic Lebanese dish with buckwheat because we love its nutty flavour and chewy texture. This salad is full of fresh herbs, which makes it a delicious summery dish. We particularly love the zing of fresh lemons, but you can take that down a notch if you prefer.

BUCKWHEAT TABBOULEH

**SERVES 2 AS A MAIN,
4 AS A SIDE**

75g roasted buckwheat
12 cherry tomatoes, quartered
30g fresh parsley, finely chopped
a handful of fresh mint leaves,
    finely chopped
3 spring onions, peeled and
    finely chopped
1–1½ lemons, juice only
3 tablespoons olive oil
salt and pepper, to taste

1. Cook the roasted buckwheat in salted water for about 10 minutes (two parts liquid to one part buckwheat). Drain if necessary, then leave to cool.
2. In a bowl, mix the cooled buckwheat with the tomatoes, parsley, mint and spring onions.
3. In a separate small bowl, mix the lemon juice, olive oil, salt and pepper, then pour over the buckwheat and combine.
4. Serve it with a fresh green salad and perhaps some flatbreads on the side.

There is no such thing as a bad potato salad in our eyes, but this recipe – donated by our German team – is really one of the best. The potatoes are sliced thin and drenched in a creamy dressing, making it an indulgent – and very pretty – side dish for barbecues, picnics and parties.

GERMAN POTATO SALAD

SERVES 4 AS A SIDE

500g small waxy potatoes
4 tablespoons vegetable oil
3 tablespoons vegan mayonnaise
2 teaspoons medium English
   mustard
2 tablespoons white wine vinegar
1 teaspoon maple or agave syrup
salt and pepper, to taste
175ml vegetable stock
½ onion, peeled and finely diced
4 pickled gherkins, halved
   lengthways, then cut into
   half-moons
a handful of fresh parsley,
   chopped
75g radishes, halved, then cut
   into half-moons

1. If the potatoes are not of uniform size, cut the larger ones in half, otherwise leave them whole. Place them in a large pan of water and bring it to the boil. Cover the pan and let the potatoes simmer away until they are cooked through but not too soft, which should be around 20–30 minutes depending on their size.

2. Meanwhile, make the dressing by mixing the oil, mayonnaise, mustard, white wine vinegar and syrup, and mix well. Season with salt and pepper.

3. When the potatoes are cooked, remove them from the heat, drain and let them cool down a bit. If the skins are thin, leave them on, but you may prefer to remove older, thicker skins at this point.

4. While the potatoes are still lukewarm, thinly slice them and place them in a large bowl.

5. Add the vegetable stock, onion, gherkins and the dressing, and leave to infuse for 10 minutes or so. Then add the parsley and radishes, mix again, season to taste, and serve.

If you're looking for a fresh twist on a pasta salad, this is the recipe for you. The roasted tomatoes and garlic combined with the basil bring a delicious taste of the Mediterranean. And this recipe is so versatile you can also serve it warm as a risotto-style main. We think you'll love it!

LEMON & ROASTED TOMATO ORZO

**SERVES 2 AS A MAIN,
4 AS A SIDE**

300g cherry tomatoes
4 whole garlic cloves, in their
    skins
olive oil
salt and pepper, to taste
200g orzo
1 lemon, zest only
10g fresh basil leaves, torn
30g roasted hazelnuts, roughly
    chopped (optional)

1. Heat the oven to 160°C fan/350°F/Gas Mark 4.
2. Place the tomatoes and garlic cloves in an ovenproof dish, drizzle some olive oil over them, and season with salt and pepper. Put them into the oven and roast for 20 minutes.
3. Meanwhile, cook the orzo in boiling water as per the packet instructions. Drain and set aside to cool.
4. When the tomatoes and garlic are soft, remove them from the oven and let them cool.
5. Squeeze the roasted garlic out of its skins and chop it up as finely as possible. In a small bowl, mix it with 3 tablespoons of olive oil and the lemon zest. Season to taste.
6. Now, combine the tomatoes and their juices with the orzo. Stir in the basil and pour the dressing over the top. Mix thoroughly to combine.
7. To serve, scatter the hazelnuts (if using) over the top for added crunch.

This is a little fancier than many rice salads, with the lovely flavours coming from orange, dill and capers, alongside the sweetness of the maple syrup. It's always a popular barbecue side, and is lovely when served over fresh green salad leaves as a meal in itself. Some supermarkets sell wild rice already mixed with another type of rice, and that will work just fine too.

BEETROOT & FENNEL WITH ORANGE WILD RICE

**SERVES 2 AS A MAIN,
4 AS A SIDE**

FOR THE SALAD
3 beetroots, peeled and cut
     into wedges
olive oil
salt and pepper, to taste
2 fennel bulbs, tough outer
     leaves removed, cut into
     wedges
1 tablespoon balsamic vinegar
150g wild rice
1 orange, peeled, segments
     separated, then cut into
     pieces
1 orange, juice only
3 tablespoons maple syrup

FOR THE DRESSING
100g plain soya yoghurt
½ orange, juice only
1 tablespoon capers
1 tablespoon chopped dill

1. Heat the oven to 170°C fan/375°F/Gas Mark 5.
2. Put the beetroot segments into a roasting dish, drizzle over some olive oil and season with salt and pepper.
3. Put the fennel into a separate roasting dish, and drizzle with olive oil and the balsamic vinegar. Mix and season.
4. Put both the beetroot and fennel dishes into the oven and roast for 40 minutes, stirring halfway through.
5. Meanwhile, cook the wild rice as per the packet instructions (usually about 25 minutes). Remove from the heat, drain and leave to cool.
6. Make the dressing by mixing the yoghurt with the orange juice, capers and dill. Refrigerate until you're ready to use it.
7. When the beetroot and fennel are cooked, remove them from the oven and let them cool. Then mix them with the wild rice and the orange segments.
8. In a small bowl, combine the orange juice and the maple syrup. Pour this over the rice and vegetables and mix thoroughly.
9. Finally, drizzle the yoghurt dressing over the top, and serve.

This salad has some of our favourite winter flavours, including chestnuts, oranges and maple-roasted pumpkin. These sweet, rich flavours alongside the natural bitterness of the chicory make a beautiful winter dish that can be served warm or cool.

WINTER SALAD

**SERVES 2 AS A MAIN,
4 AS A SIDE**

4 heads of chicory
olive oil
salt and pepper, to taste
300g pumpkin or butternut squash, deseeded, peeled and cut into 1cm cubes
2 tablespoons maple syrup
1 tablespoon sesame oil
½ teaspoon ground cinnamon
180g cooked chestnuts, roughly chopped
2 tablespoons pine nuts
1 orange, peeled, segments separated, then cut into pieces
25g walnuts, broken up
1 tablespoon fresh thyme leaves

1. Heat the oven to 170°C fan/375°F/Gas Mark 5.
2. Quarter the chicory lengthways and place in a roasting tin. Drizzle with olive oil and season with salt and pepper.
3. Place the pumpkin cubes in a bowl and add the maple syrup, 1 tablespoon of olive oil, the sesame oil and cinnamon. Mix well.
4. Put the pumpkin into a separate roasting tin and put both vegetables into the oven for 30–35 minutes.
5. Halfway through cooking, turn the chicory over, and add the chopped chestnuts to the pumpkin.
6. Meanwhile, in a hot dry non-stick frying pan, toast the pine nuts. Keep them moving to prevent them burning – they should be golden in less than a minute. Tip them into a bowl to stop them cooking further, and set aside.
7. Remove the pumpkin, chestnuts and chicory from the oven once the pumpkin is soft. Let them cool a little, then mix with the orange segments and walnuts, and top with the toasted pine nuts and the thyme leaves. Season to taste.

Check out this beautiful 1970s throwback dish! At parties back then, everything was served in, on, under or stuck into pineapples. Ah, they were simpler times. This up-to-date sweet and tangy salad can also be made using tinned pineapple and served in bowls if you're not digging that nostalgic vibe.

RAINBOW PINEAPPLE SALAD

SERVES 2

100g cooked quinoa or another grain (if you're cooking from dried, use about 35g)
50g tahini
2 limes, juice only
½ teaspoon ground cumin
½ teaspoon chilli powder (optional)
1 ripe pineapple
75g cooked green lentils (tinned is fine)
¼ red onion, finely chopped
50g red cabbage, finely shredded
1 carrot, grated
a handful of fresh coriander or parsley, chopped
a sprinkle of dried chilli flakes (optional)

1. Cook the quinoa as per the packet instructions. Set aside to cool.
2. Meanwhile, make the dressing. In a small bowl, combine the tahini, lime juice, cumin and chilli powder (if using), then add a tablespoon or two of water to loosen the mixture. Set aside.
3. Cut the pineapple in half lengthways. Scoop out the insides with a teaspoon and discard the woody core.
4. Cut the pineapple flesh into small pieces and put them into a large bowl. Mix in the cooled quinoa, and add the lentils, red onion, red cabbage and carrot. Stir in the tahini dressing.
5. To serve, load the filling back into the pineapple halves and sprinkle the fresh herbs and dried chilli flakes (if using) over the top.

This is a salad you can whip up in just a few minutes, but it is so full of flavours that it seems like you've worked harder than you actually have. It makes a popular picnic and barbecue dish, and it can be squished into a tub for a filling packed lunch.

SPICED CHICKPEA SALAD

**SERVES 2 AS A MAIN,
4 AS A SIDE**

3 tablespoons tahini
1 lemon, juice only
1 teaspoon ground cumin
1 teaspoon cayenne
1 teaspoon salt
2 x 400g tins of chickpeas, drained and rinsed
½ red onion, peeled and finely diced
½ red pepper, deseeded and diced
¼ cucumber, diced
50g watercress
a handful of fresh mint leaves, finely chopped

1. Make the dressing by mixing together the tahini, lemon juice, cumin, cayenne and salt. You may need to loosen it with a little water.
2. Put the chickpeas, red onion, red pepper and cucumber into a large bowl and pour the dressing over the top, stirring to coat everything fully.
3. Serve the chickpeas on top of the watercress and sprinkle over the chopped mint leaves.

5

DIPS

Also known as muhammara, this Middle Eastern dip, originally from Syria, has found its way into Greek cuisine and beyond. It is a little fiddly to make, but is definitely worth the effort. Not only is it very pretty, but it is perfect with warm flatbreads, on crackers, or to dip your fresh veggies into. In fact, we'd probably eat it with anything!

ROAST RED PEPPER & WALNUT DIP

SERVES 4

125g shelled walnuts
2 red peppers, halved and deseeded
6 tablespoons olive oil
1 garlic clove, peeled and minced or grated
2 tablespoons tomato purée
2 tablespoons pomegranate molasses (optional)
75g breadcrumbs
1 teaspoon ground cayenne
½ teaspoon ground cumin
1 teaspoon salt

1. Heat the oven to 180°C fan/400°F/Gas Mark 6.
2. Put the walnuts on a baking tray and let them toast for 7–8 minutes. Set aside.
3. Increase the oven temperature to 210°C fan/450°F/Gas Mark 8. Brush the red peppers with 2 tablespoons of the olive oil and roast them cut side down for 25 minutes, then turn them over and roast for another 10 minutes. Don't worry if they're charred – that's all good.
4. Carefully (they are hot!) put the peppers into a plastic bag if you have one spare, and seal it. It will steam, loosening the skins, which you can then remove to get rid of the bitter taste.
5. Put the peppers, walnuts, garlic, tomato purée, pomegranate molasses, breadcrumbs, cayenne, cumin and salt into a food processor and add the remaining 4 tablespoons of olive oil. Blitz until smooth.
6. Store in an airtight container, refrigerate and use within 2–3 days. Serve at room temperature.

If you need a spread for your crackers or a dip for your carrot batons and you need it fast, this is the recipe for you. It's a veganised version of the classic French recipe, with our own little twist – orange zest instead of lemon juice, but you could use either. If you've got guests coming over, sprinkle some chopped parsley on the top and they'll think you're a culinary genius.

ZESTY OLIVE TAPENADE

SERVES 4

200g pitted black olives
1 garlic clove, peeled and
    minced or grated
2 tablespoons capers
1 orange, zest only
50ml olive oil
black pepper, to taste

1. Put all the ingredients into a blender and pulse until you get a textured dip. (If you want more of a loose spread than a thick dip, you can drizzle in a little more olive oil.)
2. Store in an airtight container, refrigerate and use within 2–3 days. This can be served at room temperature or straight from the fridge.

If there is one ingredient that gets vegans irrationally excited, it's nutritional yeast, also known as *nooch*. It's a flaky substance that is a little bit cheesy, a little bit nutty, and is often fortified with B vitamins, making it a handy and nutritious accompaniment for pasta dishes, soups, stews, and to sprinkle on scrambled tofu for breakfast. It works wonders in this rich and cheesy dip.

QUESO

SERVES 4

150g cashew nuts
100g red pepper, deseeded and roughly chopped
4 tablespoons nutritional yeast
½ teaspoon garlic powder
½ teaspoon onion powder
½ teaspoon ground turmeric
½ teaspoon smoked paprika
a pinch of salt
100ml vegetable stock

1. If your blender is not super-high power, you'll want to soak the cashews in hot water for 30 minutes, then drain them.
2. Put all the ingredients into the blender and blitz until smooth.
3. Serve warm with tortilla chips or your choice of dunkable snacks.

This is such a simple dish that you'll want to make it for every barbecue you host, as a side to Mexican dishes, as a standalone summer salad, or to accompany tortilla chips for an in-front-of-the-TV snack.

MANGO SALSA GUACAMOLE

SERVES 4

2 ripe medium avocados, peeled and stones removed

1 ripe mango, peeled and stone removed

1 small red onion, peeled and finely diced

5–10g fresh coriander, finely chopped

1 green chilli, deseeded and finely chopped

½ lime, juice only

salt, to taste

1. Chop the avocados and mangoes into small pieces and place them in a bowl. (You can always smoosh up the avocado with a fork before you add the mango if you like it to be more of a dip and less of a salsa.)
2. Add the rest of the ingredients and mix to combine.
3. Serve in a large bowl with a big supply of tortilla chips.

A note on chillies: The standard chillies available in supermarkets often have little heat. If you prefer more, try finger or bird's-eye chillies, and if you want still more, leave the seeds in! If you like less heat, use fewer or milder chillies.

Hummus-eating vegans are a bit of a cliché, but we cannot deny the truth in it. However, there is hummus and then there is *hummus*, and this pretty dip is a fresh new twist on the much-loved classic. Ready in minutes, it's a perfect side for summertime barbecues, as an addition to salads, or just because.

MINTED PEA HUMMUS

SERVES 4

1 x 400g tin of chickpeas,
    drained and rinsed
150g frozen peas, thawed
1 tablespoon tahini
2 garlic cloves, peeled and
    roughly chopped
½ lime, juice only
2 tablespoons fresh mint,
    chopped
a good glug of olive oil
salt and pepper, to taste

1. Put all the ingredients into a blender and blitz, adding a little more oil or a dash of water to get the texture you like.
2. Store in an airtight container, refrigerate and use within 2–3 days.

6.

SOUPS & BREADS

If you like big flavours in a hearty bowl, this ramen is going to be right up your street. It's our go-to recipe for a nourishing, nutrient-packed meal, and it is easily adaptable, so you can use whatever veg you may have in your refrigerator.

RAMEN

SERVES 4

1 large onion, peeled and diced
2 tablespoons sunflower oil
2 garlic cloves, peeled and
    minced or grated
4cm piece of fresh ginger, peeled
    and grated
25g dried shiitake mushrooms
1 litre vegetable stock
2 tablespoons miso paste
3 tablespoons soy sauce
200g ramen or rice noodles
250g smoked, marinated or
    flavoured tofu, diced
1 head of pak choi, quartered
2 carrots, cut into julienne strips
    (like matchsticks)
2 tablespoons sesame oil

TOPPINGS (CHOOSE ANY/ALL)
50g beansprouts, washed
1 sheet of nori, crumbled
a handful of fresh coriander,
    chopped
2 spring onions, finely sliced
1 teaspoon chilli flakes

1. To make the broth, fry the onion in the oil until softened, then add the garlic and ginger and cook for another 2–3 minutes, stirring to prevent sticking.
2. Add the mushrooms, stock, miso and soy sauce, and bring to the boil. Reduce the heat to a simmer and cook, covered, for 15 minutes, to allow the flavours to come through.
3. Strain the liquid into a clean pan, retaining the mushrooms, but discarding the onions, garlic and ginger pulp. Slice the mushrooms and set aside.
4. Cook the noodles as per the packet instructions and add to the broth.
5. Add the mushrooms, tofu, pak choi and carrots, then bring back to the boil and simmer for another 2–3 minutes. Stir in the sesame oil.
6. Serve topped with beansprouts, nori, fresh coriander, spring onions and/or chilli flakes.

If you like your cocktails a little more warming and nourishing, this is the recipe for you. All the flavours of bloody Mary – the tomatoes, Worcestershire sauce, lemon, Tabasco and vodka – in a hearty, delicious soup. You can create the Virgin Mary version simply by leaving out the vodka; it's still very tasty and a delicious twist on the classic tomato soup. Just go easy on the Tabasco if you don't like the heat.

BLOODY MARY SOUP

**SERVES 4 AS A STARTER,
2 AS A MAIN**

3 sticks of celery, finely chopped
1 tablespoon olive oil
2 x 400g tins of tomatoes
2 tablespoons vegan
    Worcestershire sauce
a pinch of celery salt
2 tablespoons vodka
a dash of Tabasco sauce
1 lemon, juice of half and zest of
    whole
black pepper, to taste
celery leaves, chopped

1. Fry the celery in the oil for 2–3 minutes, then add the tinned tomatoes, vegan Worcestershire sauce, celery salt, vodka and 250ml of water.
2. Bring to the boil, then cover and reduce to a simmer for 10–15 minutes, until the celery is soft.
3. Remove from the heat and add the Tabasco sauce and the juice of half the lemon. Season with black pepper.
4. Blend until smooth and serve garnished with celery leaves and lemon zest.

Most supermarkets sell dried wild mushrooms, which makes them a perfect store cupboard standby for when you want to boost a meal with their characteristic umami flavour. This soup can be made just with common or garden mushrooms, and it will still be tasty, but add their wild cousins and those flavours are suddenly turbo-charged. Just remember to set aside time to soak them first.

CREAMY DILL & WILD MUSHROOM SOUP

SERVES 4 AS A STARTER, 2 AS A MAIN

35g dried porcini or shiitake mushrooms
1 onion, peeled and roughly chopped
2 tablespoons sunflower oil
500g chestnut mushrooms, cleaned and roughly chopped
2 garlic cloves, peeled and minced or grated
1 teaspoon paprika
1 medium potato, peeled and roughly chopped
850ml vegetable stock
50ml vegan cream, plus a little more for artistic drizzling
a squeeze of lemon juice
2 tablespoons fresh dill, chopped
salt and black pepper, to taste

1. Cover the dried mushrooms with boiling water and let them soak for 40 minutes to rehydrate. When soft, drain and roughly chop them, reserving the liquid.
2. Fry the onion in the oil until softened – about 7–8 minutes. Add the chestnut and porcini/shiitake mushrooms, garlic and paprika, and cook for another 3–4 minutes, stirring when necessary.
3. Add the potato, stock and the mushroom soaking liquid, and bring the soup to the boil. Cover and reduce the heat. Simmer for 10–12 minutes, or until the potato has softened, then remove from the heat.
4. Transfer to a blender and blitz until smooth.
5. Stir in the vegan cream, lemon juice and dill, and season with salt and black pepper. Gently reheat without boiling before serving, and add a swirl of vegan cream if you're out to impress.

This soup is fully loaded, not just with the sweet earthy flavour of celeriac, but also with all the extras you could heap on to a bowl of soup! It's an autumnal favourite of ours, but there is no bad time to tuck into a bowl of this naturally creamy delight. If you want a deeper, sweeter flavour you can roast the celeriac first and, if making croutons is a step too far for you, you can buy them in most supermarkets.

CELERIAC SOUP WITH GARLIC CROUTONS

SERVES 4 AS A STARTER, 2 AS A MAIN

FOR THE CROUTONS
2 tablespoons vegan butter
2 tablespoons olive oil
2 garlic cloves, peeled and minced or grated
1 tablespoon finely chopped fresh parsley
salt and pepper, to taste
200g unsliced bread (any kind except ciabatta), cut into 2cm cubes

FOR THE SOUP
1 onion, peeled and finely chopped
2 tablespoons olive oil
2 garlic cloves, peeled and minced or grated
750g celeriac, peeled and roughly chopped
1 potato, peeled and roughly chopped
1 sprig of fresh rosemary, whole
1 bay leaf
1 litre vegetable stock

TO SERVE (OPTIONAL)
fresh parsley, chopped
25g roasted hazelnuts, chopped
dried chilli flakes

1. First make the croutons. Heat the oven to 180°C fan/400°F/Gas Mark 6.
2. Melt the vegan butter in a pan and add the oil, garlic and parsley. Stir and season well.
3. Add the bread cubes and turn them over in the pan, ensuring an even coating.
4. Spread them out in a single layer on a baking sheet and cook for 15–20 minutes, until golden and crunchy. Remove from the oven and set aside to cool.
5. Meanwhile, make the soup. In a large pan, fry the onion in the olive oil until softened. Add the garlic and cook for another minute or two, stirring to prevent the garlic from burning.
6. Add the celeriac, potato, rosemary, bay leaf and stock, bring to the boil, then cover and reduce to a simmer for 25–30 minutes, until the vegetables are soft.
7. Take the soup off the heat and remove the bay leaf and rosemary sprig, then blend the soup until smooth.
8. Serve with chopped parsley, hazelnuts and chilli flakes, and with the croutons scattered on top.

This beautiful creamy soup is wonderfully warming on an autumn day. You can dial up the heat with additional chillies or let the other Thai flavours do the work. If you want the sweetness of the pumpkin to really shine, try roasting it first. If pumpkin is not available, butternut squash does the same thing, and even frozen will work just fine.

PUMPKIN THAI-SPICED SOUP

SERVES 6

1 medium onion, peeled and
　　finely diced
3 tablespoons olive oil
1 garlic clove, peeled and
　　minced or grated
2cm piece of fresh ginger, peeled
　　and grated
3 tablespoons vegan Thai red
　　curry paste
1 or 2 red chillies, deseeded
　　and finely chopped (optional
　　– if additional heat is
　　required)
1kg pumpkin, peeled, deseeded
　　and diced
400ml coconut milk
600ml vegetable stock
salt and pepper, to taste
2 tablespoons lime juice
fresh coriander, chopped, to
　　garnish
vegan cream, to garnish
　　(optional)

1. In a large pan, fry the onion in the oil until soft – about 8–10 minutes.
2. Add the garlic, ginger, Thai curry paste and chillies (if using) and cook for another 2–3 minutes.
3. Add the diced pumpkin, coconut milk and vegetable stock and bring to the boil, then cover, reduce the heat, and simmer for 20 minutes.
4. Remove from the heat and blitz the soup in a blender until smooth. Season with salt and pepper.
5. Add the lime juice, reheat gently in a pan, and serve with the fresh coriander sprinkled on the top and a swirl of vegan cream (if using).

A note on chillies: The standard chillies available in supermarkets often have little heat. If you prefer more, try finger or bird's-eye chillies, and if you want still more, leave the seeds in! If you like less heat, use fewer or milder chillies.

There is some disagreement about what constitutes a 'superfood' but there are a few foods that crop up on just about every list – foods like kale, garlic, tomatoes, beans and lentils, herbs and spices, nuts, seeds and olive oil. So we've combined all these into one very satisfying, very wholesome, chunky, souper-delicious super-soup.

SOUPERFOOD SOUP

SERVES 4 AS A STARTER, 2 AS A MAIN

FOR THE TOPPING
a handful of fresh mint leaves
½ teaspoon dried chilli flakes
1 tablespoon toasted almonds
    (or another nut)
1 tablespoon pine nuts (or
    another seed)
¼ teaspoon salt

FOR THE SOUP
2 tablespoons olive oil
1 onion, peeled and roughly
    chopped
2 garlic cloves, peeled and
    grated or minced
2 teaspoons ground cumin
1 teaspoon ground turmeric
2 x 400g tins of chopped
    tomatoes
500ml vegetable stock
50g dried red lentils, rinsed
150g tinned kidney beans,
    drained and rinsed
25g kale, shredded and woody
    stalks discarded
black pepper, to taste
½ lemon, juice only

1. In a blender, blitz the mint leaves, dried chilli flakes, almonds, pine nuts and salt until they are fully combined. Set aside.
2. Heat the oil in a large pan and gently fry the onion until it is softening – about 8 minutes.
3. Add the garlic, cumin and turmeric and fry for another couple of minutes.
4. Add the tinned tomatoes and stock, bring to the boil, then add the lentils. Cover, reduce the heat and simmer for 10 minutes.
5. Stir in the kidney beans and kale, cover again, and simmer for another 8–10 minutes. Season with black pepper to taste.
6. When the lentils are cooked, remove from the heat and serve. Add a squeeze of lemon to each bowl, with a little heap of your minty nut mix on top.

We love these flavourful savoury scones as an accompaniment to soups, or just as they are, spread with a little vegan butter. They're great for picnics and packed lunches, too, or just as an afternoon pick-me-up when lunch is all but forgotten and dinner is still too far away.

CHEESE, SPINACH & PINE NUT SCONES

MAKES 6

225g self-raising flour, plus a little more to dust the surface
1 teaspoon baking powder
1 teaspoon smoked paprika
2 teaspoons garlic powder
2 teaspoons onion powder
a pinch of salt
55g vegan butter
125g melting vegan cheese, grated, plus a little more for the tops of the scones
a handful of spinach, finely chopped
25g pine nuts
120ml plant milk, plus a little more to glaze the tops of the scones

1. Heat the oven to 200°C fan/425°F/Gas Mark 7 and put a baking sheet inside to heat up.
2. Sieve together the flour, baking powder, smoked paprika, garlic powder, onion powder and salt.
3. Rub in the vegan butter, using your fingertips, until it looks like fine breadcrumbs.
4. Stir in the grated cheese, chopped spinach and pine nuts. Then, using a metal knife, stir in the plant milk until it is fully combined into a dough.
5. Dust the work surface with flour and work the dough into a piece 1.5cm thick. Using a 6–7cm cutter, cut out the scones.
6. Remove the baking sheet from the oven and put the scones on it. Glaze the top of each scone with a little more milk and add a sprinkle more grated cheese.
7. Bake for 15–18 minutes, until golden. Serve warm or cold.

This wholesome, flour-free Irish-style bread couldn't be simpler to make. There's no kneading, no setting it aside for hours to rise. Just mix everything together and put it into the oven. It has a lovely oaty taste and a dense, satisfying texture. Not only is it a great accompaniment to soup, it is also delicious served with dips.

PORRIDGE BREAD

SERVES 6–8

400g rolled oats
1 teaspoon baking powder
1 teaspoon salt
500g plain soya yoghurt
1 tablespoon black treacle
40–50ml plant milk
20g mixed seeds

1. Heat the oven to 180°C fan/400°F/Gas Mark 6.
2. Combine the oats, baking powder and salt in a bowl, then thoroughly mix in the yoghurt.
3. Stir in the treacle, then add the plant milk to loosen the dough a little.
4. Grease a bread tin (around 18 x 11cm) and heap the mixture in. Press into the corners and smooth the top.
5. Scatter over the seeds.
6. Bake for 40–45 minutes, or until a skewer comes out clean.
7. Let it cool a little before slicing.

These absolutely delicious Chilean spicy flatbreads are cooked in a dry pan on the stove. And that means you can have warm homemade bread super fast. It's true that you'll have to knead the dough for 10 minutes first, but you can count that as an upper body workout and tick it off your to-do list. You are rocking today.

CHILEAN CHURRASCAS FLATBREAD

SERVES 6

500g plain flour
½ teaspoon baking powder
½ teaspoon bicarbonate of soda
2 tablespoons salt
2 tablespoons cayenne
2 tablespoons chilli powder
150ml warm water
100ml vegetable oil

1. In a bowl, mix together the flour, baking powder, bicarbonate of soda, salt and spices. Set aside.
2. In a jug, mix the warm water with the oil. Pour into the bowl of dry ingredients and mix to a soft dough.
3. Knead for 10 minutes.
4. Now, divide the dough into 6 portions and give each a domed, bun-like shape. Flatten each one with the palm of your hands so it has a diameter of around 10cm.
5. Pierce each churrasca with a fork several times on both sides, then put them into a hot non-stick frying pan over a medium heat and cook them for 5 minutes on each side.
6. Wait a few minutes for your churrascas to cool before serving.

These cute little breads are perfect for dunking into soups or eating with any of the dips you'll find on pages 152–158. They're also very portable and pack easily for lunchboxes and picnic baskets.

BRAZILIAN SWEET POTATO DOUGH BALLS

MAKES 12

300g peeled sweet potatoes
200g plain flour
1 teaspoon dried yeast
salt, to taste
5 tablespoons sunflower oil

1. Boil the sweet potatoes in water until soft, then drain and mash until they have the texture of a purée. Set aside.
2. Heat the oven to 200°C fan/425°F/Gas Mark 7.
3. In a bowl, mix together the flour, yeast and salt. Set aside.
4. Put 50ml of water and the oil into a pan and bring to the boil. Remove from the heat and pour it over the flour. Mix well.
5. Add the sweet potato and mix again until you have a dough.
6. Line a baking tray with baking parchment. Using your hands, form the dough into 12 balls and place them on the tray. If they are very sticky, dust some extra flour on your hands.
7. Bake for 35–40 minutes, or until the dough balls are golden and cracked on the outside.
8. Eat them warm or cool.

7.

DESSERTS

Invented only in the 1970s, it's hard to imagine there was life before banoffee pie. It's rich, sweet, creamy and dreamy, and has become an all-time classic British pud. For those who love the idea but not the bananas, you should know we just invented the Strawboffee Pie. And it was also delicious.

BANOFFEE PIE

SERVES 8

350g soft pitted dates
250g digestive biscuits
120g vegan butter, melted
250ml whippable vegan cream
    (not single or double, make
    sure it is whippable!)
2 tablespoons caster sugar
1 teaspoon vanilla extract
3 tablespoons smooth almond
    butter
3 ripe bananas, sliced into even
    rounds
your choice of vegan chocolate,
    grated, to decorate

1. Soak the dates for 10 minutes in boiling water, then drain.
2. To make the base, blitz the biscuits in a food processor until they are fine crumbs, then combine them well with the melted vegan butter. Press the biscuits into the bottom of a 24cm pie dish and place in the refrigerator to set.
3. Whip the cream in a food mixer along with the caster sugar and ½ teaspoon of vanilla extract – this can take up to 10 minutes. Set aside when stiff peaks form.
4. Make sure none of the dates contain stones still, then put them into a food processor and blitz. When the dates have formed a paste, add the almond butter and the other ½ teaspoon of vanilla extract, and process until smooth. You may need to add a tablespoon of water to get a smooth consistency. Spread this over the base.
5. Layer half the sliced bananas on to the caramel, cover with the cream, and top with the other half of the bananas.
6. Sprinkle the chocolate shavings over the top. Refrigerate for another 30 minutes, if needed, to ensure the pie is fully set.

Just wait for the *oohs* and *aahs* when you bring out this beautiful cheesecake! It's a simple recipe that requires no baking, but it is so popular and so delicious, we'd be very surprised if you did not come back for seconds.

CHOCOLATE ORANGE OREO CHEESECAKE

SERVES 8

2 packs of Oreo original
    sandwich biscuits (28
    biscuits)
60g vegan butter, melted
125g dark chocolate, broken up
50g coconut oil
450g plain vegan cream cheese
150g caster sugar
2 oranges, zest only
½ lemon, juice only

1. Place 22 Oreos (around a pack and a half) in a food processor and blitz to fine crumbs.
2. Stir in the melted vegan butter, mix thoroughly, then press firmly into a 20cm springform cake tin. Pop the cheesecake base into the refrigerator while you make the filling.
3. Melt the chocolate and coconut oil in a bowl set over a pan of gently boiling water. Make sure they are well combined.
4. Meanwhile, put the cream cheese, sugar, orange zest and lemon juice into the processor and blend until creamy. Add the melted chocolate and coconut oil and pulse to thoroughly combine.
5. Roughly break up 4 more of the biscuits and add them to the mixture. Then spread your topping over the base, using the back of a spoon to cover it evenly. Refrigerate for 2–3 hours.
6. When the cheesecake has set, crumble the last 2 biscuits over the top to serve.

Picking blackberries is surely one of life's great pleasures, and taking them home to cook them in a crumble only adds to the joy. We love this recipe, with its crunchy apples and nutty topping, and like to serve it warm, with vegan vanilla ice cream. Perfection.

BRAMBLE & APPLE CRUMBLE

SERVES 4

FOR THE FRUIT

400g cooking apples, peeled, cored and diced (about 3 large apples)
½ lemon, juice only
30g vegan butter
30g brown sugar
150g blackberries, washed
¼ teaspoon ground cinnamon

FOR THE CRUMBLE TOPPING

100g ground almonds
100g hazelnuts, chopped
65g plain flour
1 teaspoon baking powder
½ teaspoon salt
120g peanut butter
4 tablespoons maple syrup
½ teaspoon almond extract

1. Put the newly cut apples into a bowl of water with the juice of ½ lemon until you are ready to use them. This will stop them going brown.
2. Heat the oven to 180°C fan/400°F/Gas Mark 6.
3. Put the vegan butter and sugar into a pan over a medium heat until the butter is melted and a lovely caramel colour.
4. Drain the apples and pat dry with a clean tea towel. Add them to the sugar and butter and cook for 2–3 minutes.
5. Add the blackberries and cinnamon, and cook for 2–3 minutes more. Spoon into a heatproof dish (or four individual ones) and set aside.
6. Make the crumble topping by mixing together the dry ingredients with your fingertips in one bowl, and the wet ingredients in another. Then add the wet to the dry. Using your fingertips, thoroughly combine until it resembles breadcrumbs.
7. Spread the crumble topping over the fruit base and press down evenly, then bake in the oven for 15–18 minutes, until golden.

It's probably the nation's most popular dessert. A pub classic, a dinner party winner, and an all-round family favourite. We are proud to present to you this deliciously moreish sticky toffee pudding. (Riotous applause.) *See photo overleaf.*

STICKY TOFFEE PUDDING

SERVES 6

FOR THE SPONGE
200g pitted dates
250ml plant milk
1 teaspoon bicarbonate of soda
115g vegan butter
115g soft brown sugar
⅛ teaspoon grated nutmeg
½ teaspoon ground ginger
½ teaspoon ground cinnamon
200g self-raising flour
6 walnut halves, optional

FOR THE TOFFEE SAUCE
100g golden syrup
150g soft brown sugar
150g vegan butter
1 teaspoon vanilla extract
100ml vegan cream

1. To make the sponge, chop the dates into quarters and put them into a small saucepan. Cover them with the plant milk and 100ml of water, and simmer until they are soft – about 8 minutes.
2. Take off the heat and stir in the bicarbonate of soda, which will froth as you add it to the date mixture. Leave it for about 15 minutes, to cool a little.
3. Heat the oven to 180°C fan/400°F/Gas Mark 6. Grease a 20 x 20cm shallow square cake tin and line with baking parchment.
4. In a large bowl, beat together the vegan butter and sugar with a wooden spoon until creamy. Add the date mixture and stir it in.
5. In a separate bowl, mix the spices into the sieved flour. Then fold the flour into the sponge mixture. When fully combined, spoon the mixture into the prepared tin.
6. Bake for 30 minutes, or until the sponge bounces back when pressed.
7. Meanwhile, make the toffee sauce. Melt the golden syrup, sugar, vegan butter and vanilla extract in a small saucepan. Let it simmer for 5 minutes without stirring.
8. Leave it to cool slightly, then stir in the vegan cream.
9. When the cake comes out of the oven, prick it all over with a fork and pour half the hot sauce over it. It should soak in. Decorate with the walnuts (if using) and serve with the rest of the sauce on the side.

Now this is our kind of pud. It tastes so amazing that people will assume you have some serious kitchen skills, although all you did was put everything into the processor and blitz it. You can omit the chilli if that's not your thing and it'll still be a winner.

COCONUT RUM CHOCOLATE POTS WITH A SPIKE OF CHILLI

SERVES 4–6

700g silken tofu
100ml maple or agave syrup
2 limes, zest only
2 teaspoons vanilla extract
2 tablespoons coconut rum
½–1 teaspoon chilli powder
   (optional)
175g dark chocolate
1 teaspoon desiccated coconut
   (optional, for decoration)

1. Press the liquid out of the tofu by putting it into a clean tea towel and wringing it out.
2. Put the tofu into a food processor with the syrup, lime zest, vanilla extract, coconut rum and chilli powder (if using). Blitz until smooth.
3. Melt the chocolate in a bowl set over a pan of gently boiling water, then add this to the processor and pulse until combined.
4. Divide the mixture between 4-6 ramekins or espresso cups, and refrigerate for at least 30 minutes, or until ready to serve.
5. Sprinkle the tops with desiccated coconut (if using) to serve.

There is something magical – and only half believable – about making meringues out of chickpea juice, and yet it works. However, unless you are an endurance athlete who has time on their hands, you will need an electric whisk, and – as the pavlova cooks low and slow – it does take a little time. But, it is absolutely worth it. The hint of rose matches the lightness of the meringue perfectly, making a real showstopper of a dessert.

RASPBERRY & ROSE PISTACHIO PAVLOVAS

MAKES 6 INDIVIDUAL PAVLOVAS

100ml aquafaba (see page 22)
¼ teaspoon cream of tartar
100g caster sugar, plus an extra
    2 tablespoons for the cream
1 teaspoon vanilla extract
1 teaspoon rose water
250ml whippable vegan cream
    (not single or double, make
    sure it is whippable!)
50g pistachios, finely chopped
200g raspberries, washed
rose petals (optional)

1. Line a baking tray with baking parchment and set aside.
2. Put a large mixing bowl into the freezer to cool for 20 minutes. When the bowl is cold, pour the aquafaba into it along with the cream of tartar, and beat using an electric whisk on high speed until soft peaks form – around 8–10 minutes.
3. Add the 100g of sugar a tablespoon at a time, with the whisk running on high speed, until stiff peaks form – about another 10 minutes.
4. Meanwhile, heat the oven to 100°C fan/210°F/Gas Mark ½.
5. When the meringue mix forms stiff peaks, add ½ teaspoon of vanilla extract and ½ teaspoon of rose water. Beat for another minute.
6. Form the mix into six circles on the baking parchment, building up the sides of each just a little, and making sure there is some space between them to allow them to spread.
7. Bake the meringues in the oven for 1 hour 45 minutes, until they are fairly firm on the top and base. Switch off the oven and leave them inside with the door closed for 2–3 hours, until they have cooled.
8. Using the electric whisk, whip the cream with the 2 tablespoons of caster sugar and the other ½ teaspoon of vanilla extract. Depending on the brand of vegan cream, this can take up to 10 minutes. Towards the end, add in the other ½ teaspoon of rose water.
9. Gently peel the meringues from the parchment. Cover each one with the cream, sprinkle on the chopped pistachios and top with fresh raspberries. Decorate with rose petals (if using) for a memorably beautiful dessert.

Note: Vegan pavlova can be a bit of a diva. It can work perfectly nine times out of ten, and then one day, it just doesn't. There is no rhyme or reason. It's just the way it is. But a suboptimal pavlova is still a marvellous thing, so if it cracks, just cover up the fissures with cream. If it falls apart, turn it into Luton Mess (like Eton Mess but everyone's invited). It will still taste delicious, and all will be well in the universe.

With just four ingredients (unless you're tempted to make your own pastry), this really couldn't be simpler, but it tastes around a thousand times better than shop-bought treacle tarts. If you don't believe us, just try it!

TREACLE TART

SERVES 6

1 sheet of ready-made
    vegan shortcrust pastry
225g golden syrup
1 lemon, juice and zest
75g white breadcrumbs

1. Line a 20cm tart tin (or six individual mini tart tins) with the pastry, prick the base in several places with a fork, then refrigerate for 30 minutes. Cut the leftover pastry into long thin strips, about 1cm wide. Set them aside.
2. Heat the oven to 180°C fan/400°F/Gas Mark 6.
3. Gently warm the syrup in a pan, then add the lemon zest and juice.
4. Remove the pastry from the refrigerator and scatter the breadcrumbs over it. Carefully pour the syrup all over the top, making sure to cover all the breadcrumbs.
5. Now use the pastry strips you cut out to form a lattice top. It's OK if it's not perfect. Rustic is fine!
6. Bake for 25 minutes, and serve warm, with vegan cream or vanilla ice cream.

This showstopper of a dessert is inspired by a traditional Argentinian dish, and absolutely tastes as good as it looks. In reality, it is sort-of-a-cake, sort-of-a-flan, but whatever you want to call it, we are sure you will love those succulent apple and caramel flavours.

CARAMELISED APPLE UPSIDE DOWN CAKE

SERVES 8

3 apples, quartered, cored and
    sliced
½ lemon, juice only
165g self-raising flour
1 teaspoon baking powder
150g brown sugar
35ml vegetable oil
125ml plant milk
1 teaspoon vanilla extract

1. Heat the oven to 170°C fan/375°F/Gas Mark 5.
2. Grease a 20cm round cake tin (either springform or a solid tin) and set aside.
3. Put the freshly sliced apples into a bowl of water with the juice of ½ lemon until you are ready to use them. This will stop them going brown.
4. In a large bowl, mix the flour, baking powder and 75g of the sugar.
5. In a jug, mix together the oil, plant milk and vanilla extract, then stir this into the dry mixture to bring it all together. Set aside.
6. In a saucepan, heat the remaining 75g of sugar with a couple of tablespoons of water over a low heat until the sugar melts and becomes a caramel.
7. Pour the caramel into the bottom of the cake tin and swirl it round so it covers the base.
8. Drain the apples and dry them roughly with a clean tea towel. Arrange them on top of the caramel. (The prettier you make the bottom layer look, the prettier your flan will be when it is cooked.)
9. Spoon the flan mix over the top of the apples, making sure it covers them evenly.
10. Bake for 30–35 minutes, until the flan is golden on top and a skewer comes out clean. Remove the tin from the oven.
11. When it is cool enough to handle, carefully place a plate over the tin and turn it over so that the apples are on top. Let the lovely caramel juices flow down into your flan, and serve when either still warm or cooled.

A popular dessert in its native Austria and Bavaria, this fluffy shredded pancake is known by many names, including Emperor's Pancake and Emperor's Mess. The grown-up version has the raisins soaked in rum, but it's sweet and delicious when made with apple juice. And the best bit? It is supposed to be broken into pieces, so there is no need for that tense pancake-flip moment. We love to eat this *Kaiserschmarrn* warm, with vegan vanilla ice cream.

EMPEROR'S PANCAKE

SERVES 4

100g raisins
5 tablespoons apple juice
50g vegan butter
200g plain flour
10g baking powder
50g brown sugar
a pinch of salt
350ml plant milk
½ teaspoon vanilla extract
vegetable oil, for frying
icing sugar, to serve

1. Put the raisins into a small bowl and add the apple juice. Cover the bowl and let the raisins soak for at least 30 minutes.
2. Melt the vegan butter in a small saucepan or in the microwave.
3. Sift the flour into a mixing bowl and add the baking powder, sugar and salt.
4. Gradually add the plant milk and vanilla extract, stirring well to remove any lumps. Stir in the melted butter, and finally fold the soaked raisins into the batter.
5. Heat the vegetable oil in a large non-stick frying pan. Pour in the batter and fry over a medium heat until the underside is lightly browned. (It's fine to cook it in two batches if you only have a small pan.)
6. Turn with a spatula and tear the pancake into pieces. Continue to fry the dough pieces until they are lightly browned on all sides, adding a little more oil if you need to.
7. Dust with icing sugar and serve warm.

This quince tart is a very popular dessert in its native Argentina, and we can see why! It is well worth seeking out quince jelly to make it, but if you can't find it, and cannot wait for it to be delivered, you can substitute another jam or marmalade.

PASTA FROLA – QUINCE TART

SERVES 8

325g plain flour
100g vegan butter
100g caster sugar
1 lemon, zest only
a pinch of salt
340g quince jelly
½ orange, juice only
75g ground almonds
2 tablespoons desiccated
    coconut

1. Make the pastry by rubbing together the flour and vegan butter with your fingertips until it resembles coarse breadcrumbs. Add the sugar, lemon zest and salt, and mix thoroughly.
2. Add just enough water to bring the dough together. Wrap in clingfilm or a reusable waxed wrap and refrigerate for 30 minutes.
3. Meanwhile, in a bowl, mash the quince jelly, adding a little orange juice or water to thin it out. Stir in the ground almonds.
4. Heat the oven to 170°C fan/375°F/Gas Mark 5.
5. Take the dough from the refrigerator and split off about one quarter of it. Roll out the larger section on a floured surface to prevent it sticking. Carefully line a 20cm pie dish with the pastry, trimming the edges, and returning any offcuts to the rest of the dough.
6. Now roll out the smaller portion of dough and cut 1cm wide strips from it.
7. Spread the quince and almond paste evenly over the top of the pastry base.
8. Create a lattice on top with the pastry strips, pressing the edges into the base to keep it from pulling apart.
9. Bake the tart in the oven for 30–40 minutes, until the pastry is golden brown.
10. Sprinkle with the desiccated coconut and let it cool before serving. Serve as it is or with vegan cream or ice cream.

These light, thin, soft and delicious crêpes are a dream with sugar and lemon, but you could also drizzle them with syrup, or serve them with whipped vegan cream and fresh fruit. The secret here is ground flax seed which, when combined with a little water, does the job of eggs in this and many other recipes. Try it!

LEMON CRÊPES

MAKES 4–6 PANCAKES

1 tablespoon ground flax seed
125g plain flour
300ml plant milk
2 tablespoons caster sugar, plus
    more for sprinkling
¼ teaspoon salt
sunflower oil
2 lemons, juice only

1. Combine the flax seed with 3 tablespoons of warm water and set aside until it has a jelly-like consistency (just a minute or two).
2. Sift the flour, then stir in the plant milk, flax seed, sugar and salt. Put it all into a blender and blitz for 10–15 seconds.
3. Heat a little oil in a non-stick pan over a relatively high heat. When hot, add half a ladle of the mixture, swirling it round to coat the base of the pan. You want the pancake to be as thin as possible.
4. Cook for 2 minutes, then flip and cook for 1 minute more.
5. Serve with a good squirt of lemon juice and a sprinkle of sugar.

This absolute classic is loved by children and adults alike. It's simple to make, so kids can enjoy helping, though the hardest part is waiting two whole hours before it has set.

ROCKY ROAD FRIDGE CAKE

MAKES 12 PIECES

150g dark or vegan milk chocolate
35g vegan butter
2 tablespoons golden syrup
150g digestive biscuits, broken into small pieces
50g mini vegan marshmallows (or larger ones cut into small pieces)
75g glacé cherries, halved
15g desiccated coconut, plus a little more for the top

1. Line a 20 x 20cm square cake tin with baking parchment and set aside.
2. Break up the chocolate and put it into a heatproof dish. Place the dish over a pan of gently boiling water until the chocolate has melted.
3. Add the butter and syrup and stir until the butter has melted and the ingredients are well combined.
4. Remove from the heat and stir in the broken biscuits, marshmallows, cherries and coconut.
5. Pour the mixture into the cake tin, making sure it is evenly spread and pressed into the corners.
6. Refrigerate for 2 hours, then cut into pieces.

8

BAKING

Is there anything more homely than baking biscuits? This is a lovely recipe – no fuss, no faffing, just mix the ingredients together and put them into the oven. And best of all, you can whip up a batch in less time than it takes you to go to the store, which means you can have cookies even more quickly.

NUTTY CHOC CHIP COOKIES

MAKES 8

75g vegan butter
40g caster sugar
1 tablespoon golden syrup
1 tablespoon peanut butter
3 tablespoons aquafaba (see page 22)
1 teaspoon vanilla extract
100g plain flour
½ teaspoon baking powder
a pinch of salt
70g vegan chocolate chips
15g chopped hazelnuts

1. Heat the oven to 180°C fan/400°F/Gas Mark 6.
2. Beat together the butter and sugar, then stir in the golden syrup, peanut butter, aquafaba and vanilla extract.
3. In a separate bowl, mix together the flour, baking powder and salt, then stir the dry mixture into the wet mixture until thoroughly combined.
4. Finally, stir in the chocolate chips and hazelnuts.
5. Line a baking tray with non-stick baking parchment.
6. Drop the mix into 8 little heaps on the baking parchment and spread them out into rough cookie shapes with the back of a spoon or your fingers. Leave some room between them, as they will spread a little as they cook.
7. Bake for 15 minutes, until they are golden. Using a spatula, carefully (the cookies will be very soft at this point) transfer them to a wire rack to cool.

This zesty, zingy sponge cake is soft and light and utterly delicious – just as it should be. It's a clear reminder that we do not have to give up on any of our favourite treats when we eat vegan. In fact, this cake is so good we considered making it a Veganuary Ambassador.

LEMON DRIZZLE CAKE

SERVES 8–10

200g caster sugar, plus
    2 tablespoons more for
    the top
175g vegan butter
225g self-raising flour
½ teaspoon baking powder
200ml plant milk
3 unwaxed lemons (zest of 2 and
    juice of all 3)
icing sugar, to dust

1. Heat the oven to 180°C fan/400°F/Gas Mark 6.
2. In a large bowl, beat together 200g of the caster sugar and the vegan butter with a wooden spoon until creamy.
3. In a separate bowl, sift together the flour and baking powder.
4. Now add a little of the flour and a splash of the milk to the sugar/ butter mix and combine. Repeat until you have added all the flour and milk and have a smooth cake batter.
5. Stir in the juice of 1 lemon and the zest of 2.
6. Pour the mixture into a greased 24cm round cake tin and bake for 45-50 minutes, until a skewer comes out clean and the edges of the cake are just starting to turn golden.
7. Meanwhile, make the drizzle by mixing together 2 tablespoons of caster sugar and the juice from the 2 remaining lemons.
8. As soon as the cake comes out of the oven, pierce the top with a cocktail stick or a fork, and pour the drizzle over – it should sink beautifully into the cake. Leave the cake in the tin to cool.
9. When cool, turn it out of the tin and dust with icing sugar before serving.

These light, sweet, fruity muffins never fail to please, and they really couldn't be easier to make. Whip up a batch right now to improve your day one hundred per cent.

BLUEBERRY MUFFINS

MAKES 8

250g plain flour
2½ teaspoons baking powder
a pinch of salt
150g light brown sugar
175ml plant milk
100ml sunflower oil
1 teaspoon vanilla extract
125g blueberries, fresh or frozen

1. Heat the oven to 170°C fan/375°F/Gas Mark 5. Place 8 muffin cases in a muffin tray.
2. In a bowl, combine the flour, baking powder, salt and sugar.
3. In a separate bowl, gently mix together the plant milk, oil and vanilla extract.
4. Stir the wet mixture into the dry, then fold in the blueberries.
5. Divide the mixture between the muffin cases.
6. Bake for 25–30 minutes, or until the tops are golden and a skewer comes out clean.
7. Allow to cool before eating.

This is a beautifully spiced teacake-type loaf, rather like banana bread, but using jam instead of bananas. It's pretty, very tasty, and could not be easier to make. Slice and eat it as it is, or spread some vegan butter on it. Delicious!

STRAWBERRY TEA LOAF

SERVES 8

200g self-raising flour
½ teaspoon baking powder
1 teaspoon ground ginger
¼ teaspoon grated nutmeg
60g vegan butter
75g soft brown sugar
25g chopped walnuts
25g sultanas
4 tablespoons strawberry jam
100ml plant milk
2 fresh strawberries, washed,
    hulled and halved

1. Heat the oven to 180°C fan/400°F/Gas Mark 6.
2. Line a loaf tin (around 20 x 11cm) with baking parchment.
3. Sift together the flour, baking powder, ginger and nutmeg in a large bowl. Then rub in the vegan butter with your fingertips until it looks like fine breadcrumbs.
4. Add the sugar, walnuts and sultanas, and the strawberry jam. Mix well.
5. Add the plant milk a little at a time and combine well. You may not need all the milk, or you may need a little more, depending on the consistency of the jam. The mix should be thicker than a batter, and able to drop softly from a spoon.
6. Spoon the mixture into the tin, pushing it into the corners and making sure the surface is level. Place the strawberry halves on top and bake for 50 minutes to an hour, until golden on top and firm to touch. A skewer inserted into the middle should come out clean.
7. Turn out on to a wire rack to cool.

Another classic British dessert that is every bit as good as the original when made vegan, perhaps even better. This one has all the elements you look for – the gentle hint of almond, the creamy frangipane layer, the sweetness of the jam, and all topped with fresh berries. In our view it needs no accompaniment, but go right ahead and cover it with vegan whipped cream, custard or ice cream if that's how you like it.

BAKEWELL TART

SERVES 8

1 sheet of ready-rolled vegan
    shortcrust pastry
75ml coconut oil, melted
120g coconut sugar
40g plain flour
75ml aquafaba (see page 22)
200g ground almonds
½ teaspoon almond extract
4 tablespoons raspberry jam
100g fresh raspberries, washed
15g flaked almonds

1. Grease a 24cm round tart tin and place the pastry over the top. Press it into the pan gently and trim the edges. Pierce the bottom with a fork in a few places, then refrigerate for an hour.
2. Heat the oven to 180°C fan/400°F/Gas Mark 6.
3. Cover the pastry with baking parchment and top it with baking beans or uncooked rice (this helps the pastry keep its shape). Bake for 15 minutes, then remove from the oven, carefully remove the parchment and baking beans/rice, and return the tart tin to the oven for 2–3 minutes to let the base become fully dry.
4. Meanwhile, make the almond frangipane. First beat together the oil and sugar. Whisk in the flour, then the aquafaba, and finally stir in the ground almonds and almond extract.
5. Remove the pastry from the oven and spread the raspberry jam over it. On top of the jam, spread the frangipane, smoothing it over with the back of a spoon.
6. Press the fresh raspberries into the frangipane, sprinkle over the flaked almonds, and bake for 35–40 minutes, until golden. Leave to cool before slicing, to allow the frangipane to set properly.

Some cakes are fiddly and temperamental. They don't rise and you're left with a chocolate brick, or they fall apart and you're left wondering what you can make out of cake crumbs. Not this recipe. Mix the dry ingredients. Mix the wet ingredients. Mix them together. Perfect every time.

EASY VEGAN CHOCOLATE CAKE

SERVES 8–10

FOR THE CAKE
200g self-raising flour
175g light brown sugar
65g cocoa powder
1 tablespoon baking powder
½ teaspoon salt
125ml oil
275ml plant milk
2 teaspoons vanilla extract
2 teaspoons apple cider vinegar

FOR THE FROSTING
150g vegan butter
200g icing sugar, sifted
3 tablespoons cocoa powder
a splash of plant milk or cream,
    if needed

TO SERVE
fresh cherries or berries, washed

1. Heat the oven to 180°C fan/400°F/Gas Mark 6.
2. In a large bowl, mix together the flour, sugar, cocoa powder, baking powder and salt.
3. In a jug, mix together the oil, plant milk, vanilla extract and vinegar.
4. Pour the wet ingredients into the dry and combine using a spoon.
5. Grease a 20cm round cake tin and pour in the mixture.
6. Bake for 25–30 minutes and test to see if a skewer comes out clean. If it does, it's cooked. If it doesn't, cook the cake for another minute or two.
7. Take the cake out of the oven and let it cool in the tin while you make the frosting.
8. Cream together the vegan butter and the sifted icing sugar with a wooden spoon, then sift in the cocoa powder and combine. Add a splash of plant milk or cream to loosen the frosting if necessary.
9. When the cake is completely cool, cover it with the frosting and pile your choice of fresh berries on top.

We love a tea loaf, and banana bread hits the spot every time. This is somewhere between a bread and a cake, and can be eaten just as it is or spread with vegan butter. There are many ways to adapt this, including adding chopped nuts or dried fruits, but the choc chip/banana combo is our own personal favourite.

CHOC CHIP BANANA BREAD

SERVES 12

2 ripe bananas
250g self-raising flour
75g brown sugar
1 teaspoon baking powder
½ teaspoon ground cinnamon
50ml vegetable oil
60ml plant milk
75g vegan chocolate chips

1. Heat the oven to 170°C fan/375°F/Gas Mark 5.
2. Grease a loaf tin measuring about 22 x 12cm.
3. Mash the bananas in a bowl with a fork and set aside.
4. In a separate bowl, mix together the flour, sugar, baking powder and cinnamon.
5. Stir in the oil, mashed banana and plant milk. Finally, fold in the chocolate chips.
6. Spoon the mixture into the loaf tin and press it into the corners. Bake for 35–40 minutes, until golden on top.
7. Remove from the oven and let the loaf cool in the tin for around 10 minutes, then turn it out on to a rack to cool completely.

Is it just us, or do flapjacks conjure up a nostalgic memory from childhood? This is a simple recipe that yields a soft and very satisfying flapjack, and despite being a dessert, it contains some useful nutrients, too. So, while we can't pretend it's a health food, the black treacle, peanut butter, oats, sultanas and dark chocolate do give a little boost to our calcium, iron and protein intake. So, go right ahead. Have another piece.

PEANUT BUTTER FLAPJACKS

MAKES 9 SQUARES

100g vegan butter
100ml golden or agave syrup
1 heaped tablespoon black
    treacle
75g light brown sugar
125g peanut butter
200g oats
100g sultanas
½ teaspoon salt
25g dark chocolate (to drizzle
    on the top, optional)

1. Heat the oven to 150°C fan/325°F/Gas Mark 3. Lightly grease a square 20 x 20cm baking tray.
2. In a pan, combine the vegan butter, syrup, black treacle, sugar and peanut butter. Heat gently, stirring, until the butter has melted and all the ingredients are combined.
3. Put the oats, sultanas and salt into a bowl, and pour the syrup mixture over them. Stir to mix thoroughly.
4. Press the mixture into the baking tray, making sure the surface is flat, and bake for 30 minutes.
5. Remove from the oven and allow to cool in the tray for a couple of minutes before cutting into squares.
6. Melt the chocolate (either in a heatproof bowl over a pan of gently boiling water or in the microwave, stirring regularly) and drizzle over the squares.
7. When the flapjacks are completely cold, remove them from the tray.

All the delicious wholesomeness of banana bread in handy individual portions. These muffins are perfect as an on-the-go breakfast, in packed lunches, or with a cup of tea.

BANANA BREAD MUFFINS

MAKES 12

2 ripe bananas, peeled
200ml plant milk
200g caster sugar
75ml sunflower oil
2 teaspoons apple cider vinegar
2 teaspoons vanilla extract
300g self-raising flour
2 teaspoons mixed spice
1 teaspoon ground cinnamon
1 teaspoon ground ginger
½ teaspoon salt
65g walnuts, chopped
icing sugar, to serve (optional)

1. Heat the oven to 200°C fan/425°F/Gas Mark 7. Place 12 muffin cases in a muffin tray.
2. In a bowl, mash the bananas until they are pulpy, then stir in the plant milk, sugar, oil, vinegar and vanilla extract. Mix well to combine.
3. In a separate bowl, sift together the flour, mixed spice, cinnamon, ginger and salt.
4. Pour the wet ingredients into the dry and mix to combine.
5. Fold in the walnut pieces and spoon the mixture carefully into the muffin cases.
6. Bake for 20–25 minutes, until golden on top and a skewer comes out clean.
7. Let the muffins stand for 5 minutes, then turn them out on to a wire rack to cool.
8. Dust with icing sugar if you like, and serve.

Carrot cake is one of the nation's favourites, and this is our much-loved version. It has a beautiful moist interior, just as it should, and is topped with zingy orange frosting. The secret ingredient? That would be the tahini, which gives the cake a rather lovely nutty flavour.

CARROT CAKE WITH ORANGE FROSTING

SERVES 8

FOR THE CAKE
300g self-raising flour
2 teaspoons baking powder
1 teaspoon bicarbonate of soda
1 teaspoon ground cinnamon
200g carrots, peeled and grated
175g light brown sugar
50g sultanas
75g walnuts, chopped
125ml sunflower oil
70g tahini
1 teaspoon apple cider vinegar
100ml plant milk
8 walnut halves, to decorate

FOR THE FROSTING
125g vegan butter
300g icing sugar
1 teaspoon orange extract

1. Heat the oven to 170°C fan/375°F/Gas Mark 5.
2. In a large bowl, sift together the flour, baking powder, bicarbonate of soda and cinnamon. Add the carrots, sugar, sultanas and walnuts, and mix.
3. In a separate bowl, mix together the oil, tahini, vinegar and plant milk.
4. Pour the wet ingredients into the dry and stir well to combine.
5. Grease a 22cm round cake tin, and pour in the mixture.
6. Bake for 45–50 minutes, or until a skewer comes out clean.
7. Meanwhile, make the frosting by beating the vegan butter with a wooden spoon until it becomes creamy.
8. Sift the icing sugar into the butter a bit at a time and beat again to incorporate. Add the orange extract and beat again.
9. When the cake is completely cool, remove it from the tin, cover with the frosting and decorate with the walnut halves.

Forget your stodgy old tooth-cracking fruit cakes. This one, made with dark ale, is unbelievably soft and light inside. It's easy to make, sweet and rich, perfect with a cup of tea on a wintry afternoon.

PORTER CAKE

SERVES 8–10

3 tablespoons ground flax seed
175g vegan butter
450g mixed dried fruit
1 orange, zest and juice
1 lemon, zest and juice
175g demerara sugar, plus
   2 tablespoons more
200ml porter or any dark ale
1 teaspoon bicarbonate of soda
300g plain flour
1 teaspoon ground cinnamon
1 teaspoon ground allspice
½ teaspoon ground ginger
¼ teaspoon grated nutmeg
10g flaked almonds

1. Put the ground flax seed into a bowl, add 9 tablespoons of warm water, and set aside for a few minutes until it has a jelly-like consistency.
2. Grease the base of a 20cm round cake tin, and line it with baking parchment.
3. Put the vegan butter, dried fruit, orange and lemon zest and juice, 175g of sugar and the ale into a large pan. Bring it slowly to the boil, stirring until the butter has melted, then simmer uncovered for 15 minutes.
4. Heat the oven to 150°C fan/325°F/Gas Mark 3.
5. Take the fruit and ale mixture off the heat and allow it to cool for 10 minutes. Then stir in the bicarbonate of soda, which will make the mixture foam up.
6. Stir in the flax seed mixture, then sift in the flour and spices. Stir well.
7. Pour the cake mixture into the cake tin and smooth it level with the back of a spoon.
8. Sprinkle 2 tablespoons of sugar and the flaked almonds over the top and bake in the oven for 75–90 minutes. (Check it after 75 minutes by inserting a skewer into the middle. If it comes out clean, the cake is done.)
9. Allow the cake to cool in the tin for 15 minutes, then turn it out on to a wire rack to cool completely.

Rock cakes are a traditional British teatime bun, usually made with cinnamon and raisins but here given a funky new makeover. They're not supposed to be gorgeously Instagrammable, but kids love making them, and we love eating them. So what if they don't win the culinary beauty pageant? They're absolutely a winner in our eyes.

CHERRY CHOCOLATE ROCK CAKES

MAKES 10

1 tablespoon ground flax seed
250g self-raising flour
1 teaspoon baking powder
125g vegan butter
85g golden caster sugar
50g cherries (glacé, cocktail or fresh), chopped
50g vegan chocolate chips
3–4 tablespoons plant milk
1 tablespoon demerara sugar

1. Heat the oven to 180°C fan/400°F/Gas Mark 6.
2. In a small bowl, mix the flax seed with 3 tablespoons of water and set aside until it has a jelly-like consistency.
3. Sift the flour and baking powder into a large bowl and mix well.
4. Rub in the vegan butter using your fingertips, until it resembles fine breadcrumbs.
5. Stir in the caster sugar, chopped cherries and chocolate chips.
6. Add the plant milk to the flax seed mixture, mix together, then add this to the dry mix.
7. Using your hands, bring everything together to form a sticky dough.
8. Drop 10 spoonfuls of the mix on to a parchment-lined baking tray, spaced a little apart. Sprinkle a little demerara sugar on top of each rock cake and put them into the oven for 20–22 minutes, or until they are golden on top.
9. Leave to cool on a wire rack.

OPTION 2: APRICOT GINGER ROCK CAKES

While testing our rock cakes, we flirted with a few different ideas and found it hard to choose between our two favourite flavours. We knew we had to pick one, but it was like choosing your favourite child. So here is another option. Use the recipe above, and just switch the cherries for chopped dried apricots, and the chocolate chips for diced crystallised ginger.

This pretty marbled cake hails from Vienna and is popular across Austria, Germany and beyond. It consists of layers of sponge cake that intermingle with sour cherries, with a custard-style top, all covered in a chocolate glaze. Yes, it does take a little time to make, but it is not difficult, and it really is a thing of beauty.

DANUBE WAVE CAKE

SERVES 10

FOR THE CAKE
400g plain flour
200g brown sugar
a pinch of salt
2 heaped teaspoons baking powder
1 teaspoon bicarbonate of soda
300ml plant milk
120ml vegetable oil
2 tablespoons apple cider vinegar
1 teaspoon vanilla extract
3 tablespoons cocoa powder
vegetable oil or vegan butter, for greasing
200g sour or morello cherries, drained

FOR THE CUSTARD
40g cornflour
50g brown sugar
400ml plant milk
1 teaspoon vanilla extract
150g vegan butter, at room temperature

FOR THE CHOCOLATE GLAZE
175g dark chocolate
30g coconut oil

1. Heat the oven to 180°C fan/400°F/Gas Mark 6.
2. In a mixing bowl, combine the flour, sugar, salt, baking powder and bicarbonate of soda.
3. In a jug, combine the plant milk, vegetable oil, apple cider vinegar and vanilla extract. Mix this into the dry ingredients.
4. Pour about half the batter into another bowl and mix in the cocoa powder.
5. Grease a 20cm round cake tin with some oil or vegan butter, then spoon in the light-coloured cake batter and spread evenly.
6. Now spoon the dark batter over the light batter, and spread it out as evenly as possible. Don't worry if it's not perfect – the layers will mix and marble.
7. Add the cherries evenly over the top. Then put the cake into the oven and bake for about 30–35 minutes, or until a skewer comes out clean. Leave it to cool in the cake tin.
8. While the cake is cooling, make the custard. In a bowl, mix the cornflour with the sugar. Stir in about 5 tablespoons of cold plant milk and the vanilla extract.
9. Put the remaining plant milk into a saucepan and bring it to the boil. Add the cornflour mixture, then reduce the heat and simmer for about 2 minutes, stirring constantly, until it thickens into a custard. Leave it to cool, stirring every now and then. Set aside.
10. In a bowl, whisk the vegan butter until it is fluffy. When the custard has cooled down to room temperature, stir it into the whisked butter. Spread this over the cooled cake and chill in the refrigerator for at least an hour.
11. Finally, make the chocolate glaze. Break up the chocolate and put it into a heatproof bowl with the coconut oil. Place it over a pan of gently boiling water until it has melted. Stir to combine, then spread the chocolate glaze carefully over the custard layer. Pop the cake back into the refrigerator for another 30 minutes to let the chocolate set.

REFERENCES

1. 'Vegan diets reduce the risk for chronic disease', Health and Nutrition News, 8 April 2019, https://www.pcrm.org/news/health-nutrition/vegan-diets-reduce-risk-chronic-disease

2. Martin, M. J., Thottathil, S. E. and Newman, T. B., 'Antibiotics overuse in animal agriculture: a call to action for healthcare providers', American Journal of Public Health, December 2015; 105(12): 2409–10, https://www.ncbi.nlm.nih.gov/pmc/articles/PMC4638249/

3. Greger, M., 'Primary pandemic prevention', American Journal of Lifestyle Medicine, September–October 2021; 15(5): 498–505, https://www.ncbi.nlm.nih.gov/pmc/articles/PMC8504329/

4. Food and Agriculture Organization of the United Nations, GHG emissions by livestock, https://www.fao.org/news/story/en/item/197623/icode/

5. Robert Goodland, 'Lifting livestock's long shadow', Nature Climate Change 3, 2 (2013), https://www.nature.com/articles/nclimate1755

6. Harvard School of Public Health, 'Healthy plant-based diets better for the environment than less healthy plant-based diets', 10 November 2022, Harvard: https://www.hsph.harvard.edu/news/press-releases/healthy-plant-based-diets-better-for-the-environment-than-less-healthy-plant-based-diets/; University of Oxford, 'New estimates of the environmental cost of food', 1 June 2018: https://www.ox.ac.uk/news/2018-06-01-new-estimates-environmental-cost-food; Chatham House, 'Food system impacts on biodiversity loss', 3 February 2021: https://www.chathamhouse.org/2021/02/food-system-impacts-biodiversity-loss; 'Plant-based diet can fight climate change – UN': BBC News, 8 August 2019, https://www.bbc.co.uk/news/science-environment-49238749

7. Rao, S. 'Animal agriculture is the leading cause of climate change. A position paper', Journal of the Ecological Society, 1 April 2021, 32–3, https://www.scienceopen.com/hosted-document?doi=10.54081/JES.027/13

8. WWF, Living planet report 2022, https://www.wwf.org.uk/our-reports/living-planet-report-2022

9. McMacken, M. and Shah, S., 'A plant-based diet for the prevention and treatment of type 2 diabetes', Journal of Geriatric Cardiology, May 2017; 14(5): 342–54, https://www.ncbi.nlm.nih.gov/pmc/articles/PMC5466941/

10. Poovorawan, Y., Pyungporn, S., Prachayangprecha, S. and Makkoch, J., 'Global alert to avian influenza virus infection: from H5N1 to H7N9', Pathogens and Global Health, July 2013; 107(5): 217–23, https://www.ncbi.nlm.nih.gov/pmc/articles/PMC4001451/; WHO, Avian Influenza Weekly Update Number 838, 1 April 2022, https://www.who.int/docs/default-source/wpro---documents/emergency/surveillance/avian-influenza/ai-20220401.pdf; UK Health Security Agency, Risk assessment of avian flu: https://www.gov.uk/government/publications/avian-influenza-a-h7n9-public-health-england-risk-assessment/risk-assessment-of-avian-influenza-ah7n9-sixth-update

INDEX

C

D

E

Q

R

S

V

W

Y

Z

WHO ARE WE?

Veganuary is a non-profit organisation that, since 2014, has encouraged people worldwide to try vegan for January and beyond. Every year, hundreds of thousands of people register to take part, but research suggests that the true participation figure could be ten times higher. Throughout the year, Veganuary supports and guides people and businesses alike to move towards a plant-based diet as a way of protecting the environment, preventing animal suffering, and improving health.

Our January campaign is the most high-profile aspect of our work, but we are active throughout the year, working with businesses to launch more and better plant-based dishes and menus, and raising the profile of veganism through traditional media and on social platforms.

We are lucky and proud to be supported by some wonderful well-known names and are indebted to our extraordinary Ambassadors for their love and support. We dedicate this book to them and to every one of our participants who was willing to try something new, and to see where it would lead them. Almost all of them tell us that they have changed how they eat as a result of that month-long challenge and would recommend taking part in Veganuary to others. That makes us very happy.

And although this book is all about creating delicious food, if you want to know more about the issues associated with veganism, or need some practical tips on becoming vegan, you can find these in our companion book *How to Go Vegan*, or follow us on social media.

Facebook @Veganuary
Instagram @WeAreVeganuary
Twitter @Veganuary

Take Part in Veganuary

It is free to sign up for our month-long vegan challenge and you can do so any day of the year, although most people start on 1 January. Over 31 days, you will receive inspirational emails with tips and tricks, facts and advice, brand new recipes, and lots more. You'll get access to our dedicated Facebook Group, where you can share your experience with thousands of others and feel part of this exciting worldwide challenge.

Find out more and sign up at Veganuary.com

THANK YOUS

This book has been possible only because of our fabulous recipe creators, donors, tasters and testers. Huge thanks go to Abigail Geer, Adam Paterson, Anastasia Sargent, Andrew Jolly, Angela Tarry, Ben Fearnside, Bree Cannon, Candice Haridimou, Carole Backler, Chelsea Harrop, Christopher Hollmann, Christopher Shoebridge, Claudia Tarry, Dan Foster, Dav Yendle, Emilie Soffe, Emma Yoxall, Felicity Crump, Graeme Wotherspoon, Jane Land, Jeff Doyle, Karen Waldron, Karimah Stroud, Kate Fowler, Kate Sims, Katharina Weiss-Tuider, Kim Waldron, Lisa Paterson, Mathew Glover, Matthew Harris, Mauricio Serrano, Nadja Lindacher, Paul Sims, Phoebe Hobbs, Prashanth Vishwanath, Robert Adams, Roy Thompson, Sofia Balderson, Soundarya Sharma, Steven West, Stuart Giddens, Susan West, Toni Vernelli, Tony Waldron, Tracy Ellen, Wendy Matthews and Zoe West.

Our thanks also to the wonderful Jane Graham Maw and the whole team at Graham Maw Christie Agency, and to the super-talented Lydia Good and the HarperCollins team.

Thorsons
An imprint of HarperCollins*Publishers*
1 London Bridge Street
London SE1 9GF

www.harpercollins.co.uk

HarperCollins*Publishers*
Macken House, 39/40 Mayor Street Upper
Dublin 1, D01 C9W8, Ireland

First published by Thorsons 2023

10 9 8 7 6 5 4 3 2 1

Text © Veganuary Trading Limited 2023
Photography © Lizzie Mayson 2023

Veganuary asserts the moral right to be identified as the author of this work

A catalogue record of this book is available from the British Library

ISBN 978-0-00-858024-7

Food Stylist: Flossy McAslan
Prop Stylist: Louie Waller
Illustrations: RioRita/Shutterstock.com

Printed and bound by GPS Group

MIX
Paper | Supporting responsible forestry
FSC™ C007454

This book is produced from independently certified FSC™ paper to ensure responsible forest management.

For more information visit: www.harpercollins. co.uk/green

WHEN USING KITCHEN APPLIANCES PLEASE ALWAYS FOLLOW THE MANUFACTURER'S INSTRUCTIONS.